The Last
SUNDAY DRIVE

The Last
SUNDAY DRIVE

VANISHING TRADITIONS IN GEORGIA AND THE CAROLINAS

TOM POLAND

THE
History
PRESS

Published by The History Press
Charleston, SC
www.historypress.com

All images are by the author.

First published 2019

Manufactured in the United States

ISBN 9781467143103

Library of Congress Control Number: 2019948142

Notice: The information in this book is true and complete to the best of our knowledge. It is offered without guarantee on the part of the author or The History Press. The author and The History Press disclaim all liability in connection with the use of this book.

CONTENTS

CONTENTS

A Sunday drive is an automobile trip, primarily in the United States and Australia, typically taken for pleasure or leisure on a Sunday, usually in the afternoon. During the Sunday drive there is typically no destination and no rush.

—*Wikipedia*

Author's Note: This book recalls that time when people devoted Sunday afternoons to visiting relatives and sightseeing. Revisit ways of life, places, institutions and people that made the 1950s, 1960s and early 1970s memorable. Sundays back then were times when folks had some free time, a time when few cars had air conditioning or seatbelts even. With this book, you can travel back to the days before air conditioning, fast food, plastic cutlery, television, interstates and information technology strangled a great tradition. A lot of folks today will tell you they find little pleasure in driving. Daily commutes, traffic jams, roads forever under construction, phone-distracted drivers, franchise restaurants and interstates ruin driving. The Sunday drive, however, lives on between the covers of this book, and here's hoping a few of us will resurrect the Sunday drive and once again find joy in aimless driving.

Introduction

'56 PLYMOUTH MEMORIES

In the 1950s, it was customary for folks to take Sunday drives. Gather up the family and see the sights. Tour the countryside. See what there was to see and visit relatives, most of whom lived close by. And then the years rolled by. That pastime, the Sunday drive, faded. Now it's a rarity. Families live all over the country, and people find themselves in a rush. "Sunday driver," however, is alive and well. In today's mad race against time, a driver who dawdles is a "Sunday driver," but dawdling was the order of the day when the drive was the destination.

In the 1950s and '60s, families would make a Sunday drive to see the land up close, banish boredom, visit family and cool off with 460 air conditioning—just roll all four windows down and drive 60 miles per hour.

Today, we live in the era of superhighways. Interstates, ever-widening highways and freeways don't give you much to see as you rush from point to point. That's driving. In Dad's aqua-white '56 Plymouth Belvedere, we journeyed. A Sunday drive felt a bit like the drives we took down Highway A1A to Florida: a departure from the ordinary, an adventure.

We had two TV stations, and as miraculous as they were, not even grainy black-and-white shows could cure the ills of a long Sunday afternoon. The countryside beckoned. A Sunday drive was the high point of the week, a wondrous escape. The ordinary? It was extraordinary, and memories remain luminous.

EASTERN GEORGIA, SUMMER 1958

With church and dinner behind me, the July afternoon looms long and empty—a vacant, blistering desert. Nothing to do, nowhere to go and all afternoon to get there. Time drags. Today feels like a month of Sundays. Our dog, Duke, sleeps beneath the house. In the dusty heat, even the cicadas refuse to sing their rising-falling singsong song. It's another sultry Sunday down South.

My lone escape? Reading. I go inside and resume reading a Hardy Boys mystery, *The Ghost at Skeleton Rock*. A getaway with Frank and Joe will have to do. Just as I start chapter 14, "The Unseen Enemy," a hood slams in the driveway. Here comes Mom with her purse. "Put your shoes on."

Out the screened porch we go to pile into Dad's car. "Where are we going?"

"Nowhere, everywhere," Dad says.

Behind the Plymouth's sleek jet-like hood ornament, we're about to take off. The newfangled push-button automatic transmission turns the dash into a cockpit. Our long dusty driveway? It's a runway. We build momentum, take off and break through the boredom barrier, smashing it to smithereens.

We roll the windows down, and the winds blow away the heat. Through town, just missing the red light. Dad turns onto a dirt road. Now our jet-car leaves a contrail of dust as we glide by mysteries. What's it like in that fire tower during a storm? Just beyond it sits an old homeplace with a cast-iron hand pump. Dad drank from it as a boy. "The water was sweet." Around a bend we pass a sawdust pile where chips glitter like sequins. Mom says, "Never play on a sawdust pile. You'll fall in and die." Not far past the death chips is a yard with tree trunks painted white. Why?

Onto a tarry, graveled road we turn, and like a dog, I stick my head out the window into summer fragrances...a field of hay, the fertile smell of pastures, a hint of honeysuckle and now and then briny swamp fragrances. And always the duct tape–ripping sound of tires rolling through molten tar.

Past more mysteries—in a green pasture, whiteface cattle stare in the same direction. That old barn on the verge of collapse. How have its nails and timbers defied gravity for decades? We motor past the little shack where Dad knows a man who eats white dirt. Dirt? White dirt? Past the farm where Old Man Bolton removes warts with a broomstraw and incantation. Past an abandoned farm where a peach tree grows through the bed of a rusty 1930s pickup truck. Does anyone pick up those peaches? Far off at the edge of a field, I see an odd tree stand. Some fellow has attached an old oil drum high up in a tree to stand in. Surely deer avoid that place.

Highway 430, Edgefield County. In the old days, the bales would have been rectangular or "square," as farmers called them.

We watch the countryside roll by and talk about landmarks and marvels: an old country store with one lonely gas pump, a chimney where a man burned his house to the ground on purpose, past a birch, white as paper, that people have carved initials into. In a field sits an old sofa with a buzzard perched on it. And there's where a girl fell into an old hand-dug well. Spent a day in it before rescue.

We see yard art of the era, truck tires converted to big flowerpots, gourds hung for purple martins, tires hanging from tree limbs, homemade swings. Sometimes Dad uses an old box camera loaded with Kodak film to take photos. Where they went is anybody's guess.

On Highway 79, I know I'll see a mule alone in a pasture, always by a fence watching traffic go by. Not even a goat to keep it company. That plebian mule has to be the loneliest creature in the South. There's the old Chennault Place, where Mom says a ragtag band of men robbed the Confederate gold train. "People still dig up the place," she tells me. The Chennault Place looks like the plantation homes in my history book. I imagine men in white suits digging for gold beneath massive oaks draped in Spanish moss—a Lowcountry plantation—something I hope to see one day.

On we drive past an old store that looks like it belongs in a Western. I half expect to see tumbleweeds blowing by. We speed downhill toward Pistol Creek, then up a steep hill. Now we spirit across a dammed river into blue granite country. "Over yonder," Mom says, "is Anthony Shoals. It was my beach when I was a girl." I look left upriver, but just then a car with fins like a shark blows past us. "'57 Lincoln Capri," Dad says.

We drive past places familiar yet foreign, homes with mailboxes atop granite posts, porch sitters I'll never meet, cornfields scorched by the sun, churches with big cemeteries and homes with family plots. These Sunday drives, they reveal the land, life and death—visions that will stay with me until I die.

ABOVE South Carolina's only See Rock City barn, Highway 28 south of Abbeville.

OPPOSITE Window units ruled in the 1950s and 1960s. AC brought change, and things like porch sitting lost their appeal.

We cross into South Carolina and drive through a place Dad calls "Saloon Falls." We follow Highway 72 to Abbeville. You can see California redwoods, sequoias, here. We turn south, and a ways out of town, I spot another barn through the rear window. "See Rock City," paling words on tin streaked with cinnamon-like rust. Beneath a shed sits a bright blue two-door Chevy of the '40s. Stacked near it are fence posts, cedar trees robbed of limbs and crowns.

Now and then we see an odd machine stuck in a home's window. Air conditioning is creeping into our southern summers. We stop at an old store where its Royal Crown thermometer registers ninety-nine degrees. Inside wait crackers in big jars with the name "Lance" on them. Next to them sit even bigger jars full of big cookies beneath red lids. Lift a lid and sweetness spices the air. Just above the crackers and cookies are shelves crammed with saltine crackers, white vinegar, baking soda, Vicks VapoRub and mineral oil. A flambeau sits next to a blue-and-white wooden ice cream churn. Dad buys a pack of Chesterfields, and we leave this place that has it all.

Late afternoon. The air, it cools; the light, it changes. The undersides of windblown leaves whiten in darkening light. "A cloud is coming up," says Dad. Through the windshield, I see thunderheads fanning spokes of smoky light toward the earth. A yellow-white fork splinters the sky. We turn onto a nameless gravel road where yet another white-shingled house stands. Out its door runs a woman to gather laundry, her long dark hair trailing in the wind. She gathers sun-dried clothes, clean, starchy and fragrant.

Raindrops big as marbles clatter against the windshield. A purple cloud spitting neon darts blows in, and the fertile smell of rain-spattered earth rises. Dad turns his two-tone, white-walled Plymouth around as we roll up the windows. Homeward bound, we are. This drive ends too soon.

***

We can thank post–World War II prosperity and a blossoming romance with cars for Sunday drives, once a treasured custom, but like porch sitting, if the Sunday drive isn't dead, it's dying. Gasoline's no longer pennies on the gallon. Air conditioning keeps folks inside, and going nowhere is the easy thing. Besides, TV channels by the hundreds hypnotize people; zombies they become. Cooking shows. Home makeovers. Murder mysteries. Come fall, pro football. And all the while, a digital culture walls them in. With heads bent over, people don't make eye contact or talk, much less make a Sunday drive together. They send text messages, private messages and e-mails, and social media let them like this, like that, share this and share that. Sharing a Sunday drive? Few do that, and so a fun, adventurous way of knowing their homeland and each other fades.

People used to make Sunday drives, and those who lived along state lines enjoyed the added thrill of entering another state. It wasn't like going abroad, but it was different. Two-state sightseers they were. James Dickey remembers those days. "In the old days, that was the only entertainment people got, was, say, like spending Sunday afternoon going and visiting people." You and I? Let's make one last Sunday drive through a vanishing Southland of old. Eastern Georgia, South Carolina entire and the South Carolina–North Carolina border shelter places where you can recapture that time when adventure waited around the curve, that time of no destination, no rush. That time when a desire to see how people lived and the land they called home drew people into the countryside. They were scholars, blue-collar historians, with a passion for the old ways, landmarks, old-timers and vestiges of how our ancestors lived.

It's not too late for you and me. The tank is full. Come. Make the last Sunday drive with me.

Tom Poland
Columbia, South Carolina
May 2019

OLD-TIMERS

When I was young, old folks made me nervous. Like preachers and teachers, they represented authority, something I dislike to this day. Still, old-timers who had survived all manner of risks, threats and life's endurance races represented treasures. As I wrote about an aunt who passed away at ninety-five, she passed through times the likes of which many of us will never see: Prohibition, the Great Depression, World War II, Japan's attack on Pearl Harbor, JFK in Dallas, Neil Armstrong setting foot on the moon. And there were hundreds upon hundreds of personal events she collected. What we call "life." Births. Deaths. Vacations. Meals. Heartbreak. Elation. Disappointment. Careers. Family. Beloved pets. The things she learned. That's why losing a loved one is like having a museum or a great library burn to the ground.

Old folks had old ways, and looking back, I sure miss the older folks and their ways I encountered in the day of the Sunday drive. A few made it to more modern times, but they kept their older ways alive, old maids and granddads among them. We're blessed to have their stories.

A SONG FOR MISS JOHNNIE

We had no train tracks where I grew up, but we did have an old maid in town, and Sundays when we passed Miss Lucy's home, I knew she was peering out the window. She lived right across from a spooky old school, the Green Building, and she didn't tolerate children in her yard. We kids knew she was not to be trifled with. Just the mention of her name sent us running.

In the years to come, I forgot about Miss Lucy, but then a curious blending of old maids, an old school friend and train tracks came my way. I learned that some old maids are sweet, lonely ladies.

***

Circa 1959: In deep country, we seldom encountered train tracks, but when a Sunday drive through Carolina paused at a crossing and a train barreled through, it thrilled me. "Count the cars," Dad would say, and count 'em I would. The engine would shoot past, its blasting horn dropping, diesel engine thrumming, cars clanking, bell a'ringing and steel wheels clattering. A beautiful, clamorous symphony to hoboes, I figured.

Some folks lived close to the tracks, though, and how on earth, I wondered, did they sleep at night. Well, one lady loved to see the trains roll by her home, even in the dead of night. Miss Johnnie lived in the heyday of the Sunday drive but didn't have to drive to see a train. No, the trains came to her.

To explain, I must turn the clock back to long-gone days in the red clay state and one Ronnie Myers, now of Abbeville, South Carolina. My abiding memory of Ronnie is hearing him sing and play guitar in his high school band, the Comets. Ronnie strummed a red electric guitar, if memory serves me right. The Comets? Well, they came of age during the British Invasion, and for a while, I thought Lincolnton, Georgia, had an answer to the Beatles.

Ronnie? He graduated and moved on. Then some fifty years later, we crossed paths. He had done something I envied: worked as a trainman. "Tell me some train stories, Ronnie; tell me some please."

Tell me he did, and among them is this lonely happy, happy lonely tale of what folks once called an old maid, Miss Johnnie O'Bryant. She lived in Auburn, Georgia, near the railroad tracks.

"We could see her house really well from our train," said Ronnie. "She lived all alone except for her cats. She literally loved our trains and us. She acknowledged every train that passed her house with a wave with her hankie by day and a flashlight by night. We all looked for her when we would go by."

***

"I hear the train a'coming, rolling 'round the bend."

"Look a-yonder comin', comin' down that railroad track, it's the Orange Blossom Special, bringing my baby back."

"Folsom Prison Blues" and "The Orange Blossom Special." Two songs from the man in black and one lonely train-loving woman. Oh, sing a train song, Ronnie, sing it through the year. Blow that horn, blow it for her to hear. Strum your guitar, strum it hard, cause Miss Johnnie someday's gonna meet the Lord...

***

Who doesn't need something to look forward to, something that gives life cadence? For Miss Johnnie O'Bryant, trains did just that. The clacking of the rails must have been music to her. She lived in a small four-room house just west of Auburn, Georgia, about one hundred yards from the railroad tracks that parallel Highway 29. "We could see her house really well from our train," said Ronnie.

Miss Johnnie loved the railroad men and their conveyances of steel. She could hear the train a'coming, coming 'round the bend. "We all looked for her," said Ronnie. "Even in the wee hours, we would see her flashlight waving from her window. We always blew the horn when we passed."

Miss Johnnie lived in lean circumstances, so the men learned. At Christmas, the trainmen, conductors and engineers would chip in some money and an old conductor friend of hers, Ben Powell, would drive to Auburn to deliver it. "Practically all one hundred or so railroad men from Abbeville would contribute about twenty dollars each," said Ronnie.

An appreciative Miss Johnnie wrote letters to the men, and they would pin her letters on the bulletin board in the crew room at the Abbeville depot. She wrote about everyday life. Her flowers and vegetable garden, her cats, the frogs in the little spring close to her yard. (She didn't have running water.) "She even had names for certain frogs," said Ronnie. "She talked a lot about her favorite radio announcer, Ludlow Porch, whom she listened to religiously every day."

Trains bring rhythm to those who live close to tracks. Miss Johnnie was one such person.

Don't know Ludlow? Well, he was one of Lewis Grizzard's stepbrothers (Bobby Crawford Hanson). Ludlow, humorist and radio talk-show host, always ended his show with, "Whatever else you do today, you find somebody to be nice to."

Ronnie certainly did. "Occasionally I would be called to cover an outlying job, and I would drive my personal car to other towns to work a switcher (an engine and crew that work local businesses). One summer day, I had gotten off work in Lawrenceville, and driving home, I decided to stop by Miss Johnnie's. I wanted to meet the lady who always waved at us."

Ronnie walked through Miss Johnnie's fragrant purple old-timey petunias, the perennial kind our southern grandmothers grew in their yards. He knocked on her screen door and waited. He waited some more, and then her visage materialized through the screen. "It startled me at first. She had a serious, cautious look, so I immediately told her my name and that I worked on the railroad and had been wanting to meet her."

A smile crossed Miss Johnnie's face, and she invited Ronnie into her front room. "We had a chat about her cats and how dry the summer was." She told Ronnie one of her cats was sick because it had eaten too many lizards. She told him she loved trains and had always lived near the tracks since she was a girl. And then music—that balm of the soul—entered the picture.

"Through the open bedroom door, I saw an acoustic guitar on her bed," said Ronnie. "'I see you play guitar.'" Miss Johnnie said she played a little bit, and Ronnie said he did too. "'Matter of fact, I have mine out in the car.'"

You could say a mini-concert took place.

Miss Johnnie had an old Sears & Roebuck Silvertone guitar. "They were really good-quality guitars back in the day before they started manufacturing cheap department store toy guitars and passing them off as real guitars," said Ronnie. "Miss Johnnie played the guitar pretty well. She sang the old tune 'On Top of Old Smoky…all covered with snow, I lost my true lover for courtin' too slow.'"

Ronnie couldn't help but feel this "old maid" was thinking of an old boyfriend while singing. Maybe so. "An old railroad friend who lived near her told me she, a sister and her mother had lived in that same old house as long as he could remember and that Miss Johnnie had taken care of them until they both died."

After some music, Ronnie left Miss Johnnie's with vegetables from her garden and a bag of dried apples she had placed on tin in that hot Georgia summer sun. "I left with a good feeling and a song in my heart," said Ronnie.

A few months later in his Atlanta motel room, a melody popped into his head. And then the words came:

Miss Johnnie O'Bryant lived by our tracks, she always waved, and we waved back
On a midnight train, we'd see her light, and she'd hear our horn blow
I stopped by one summer day; her flowers smelled sweet in a strange purple haze
This lady loved trains like her flowers loved dew
She lived all her life in this small Georgia town reading her Bible and tilling the ground
When she leaves this world, full of sorrow and pain, when she goes to heaven, she'll go on a train
She said I could have married a long time ago, I could have said yes, but always said no
I'd rather live all alone just to hear those old trains and their big engines moan

We who ride these rails every day, sure miss our families in so many ways
But just a wave in the passing, a how do you do, sure eases our sadness, it's the least she could do
She lived all her life in this small Georgia town, reading her Bible and tilling the ground
When she leaves this world full of sorrow and pain, when she goes to Heaven she'll go on a train
When Johnnie sees Jesus, she'll be on a train

Ronnie saw Miss Johnnie one more time. He stopped by, sang her song to her and gave her the lyrics. And then those trains rolled on and so did time. Lots of time. The day came when they moved Miss Johnnie to a nursing home in downtown Winder. Fate was kind, however. The home sat just across Highway 29 from the tracks. Said Ronnie, "From then until I left the railroad, when we came through Winder, no matter what time of day or night, I'd blow our horn loud and long because I knew she'd be listening."

Oh, sing that train song, Ronnie...sing it through the year. Blow that horn, blow it loud for her to hear. Strum your guitar, strum it hard, cause Miss Johnnie, she's wandered off to meet the Lord...

***

In 2005, many years after he left the railroad, Ronnie learned Miss Johnnie O'Bryant had passed away. She rests in a cemetery in Winder. "I hope to go by her grave someday," said Ronnie.

Well, at least her home and petunias still stand across from the tracks. Right? Well, no. "I heard her little four-room house was torn down and an appliance store was built at that location," said Ronnie, "but to us older railroad guys, Miss Johnnie O'Bryant will always be there."

She will.

People pass on, but their presence remains. A fragrance, a song—why, even a sound brings them back. "Hey, buddy, do you hear that horn? Look a-yonder comin,' comin' down that railroad track. It's Ronnie and the trainmen bringin' Miss Johnnie back."

GRANDDAD'S '65
COW-CHARMING CHEVY

Granddad Poland, Mr. Johnny, never took a Sunday drive that I know of. He farmed but never drove a pickup, not that I recall. Come sundown in a battered old car, he'd bump through pastures festooned with yellow bitter weeds, clunk past a lonely persimmon tree and ranks of white-faced cattle. Herefords, they were. From afar, those cows would amble Granddad's way, and when his jalopy closed in, they would break into a stiff-kneed trot. To see the old man's car was to see feed. And to see the cattle rushing toward an old-time farmer was a sight we often saw on Sunday drives. Not so much anymore. Farming has progressed too.

I remember, though, how my best friends, the children of field hands, and I sat in the back of Mr. Johnny's cars. Sometimes we rode on the trunk, sometimes on the fenders. We were invincible and we were oblivious. The era of Jim Crow was upon us, but Joe Boy, Sweetie, Jabe and I knew nothing about all that. We were comrades in arms united in our quests to knock down red wasp nests, catch bluegills, dine on tomato-red persimmons and swim in ponds sometimes blue, sometimes muddy.

Granddad wore a felt hat and overalls. He didn't tolerate fools. Whenever I was in his presence, I felt the need to hush up. Mr. Johnny didn't talk much, so neither did I. And maybe that was good. Memories of drives through pastures about lightning bug time please me still. The grassy slopes…the fertile fragrance of pastures…the lowing of cattle… the distant line of dark trees that seemed an artist had sketched it and fishponds smooth as glass where bullfrogs commenced to sing and fireflies lit up green clumps of rushes.

When the car shut down with a shudder and we sat still as stones, country sounds embraced us: wind, lowing cattle, the distant hoot of a barred owl. Nary an ambulance, firetruck or police siren. *Sigh-reen*, as the country folk are wont to say. "Did y'all hear that sigh-reen last night?"

Most of what pleased me as a boy took place on that farm. And so I associate Granddad's old cars with treasures—varnished cane poles, red-and-white bobbers, mats of algae that betrayed snakes' serpentine wanderings, jelly-like clumps of frog eggs and the heavy wooden boat Granddad made with ever-present snakes beneath—treasures like no others.

Grandmom taught me to dig worms from beneath cow piles. We marveled at a great pine of another epoch that served as a place to butcher cattle. We tread by it with reverence. That farm was our Disneyland, and Granddad's old car carried us o'er its pastures, bottoms and woodlands. We were kings in a kingdom where palatial riches waited around the bend of every cow path.

When we were on foot, away from Granddad, we sought mischief. There was a time when a western section of Granddad's pasture looked like a junkyard. Old cars, old tractors, farm implements and all manner of scrap metal gave red wasps places to hang their waxy papery nests, which we gleefully clobbered with flint rocks. The fun part? Running for your life when a boiling ball of mad wasps shot out.

I'd do it all again.

It's a damn shame we grow up. By the time I was in college and too big for my britches, Granddad used a 1965 Chevrolet Bel Air as his truck. It would be his last. A green copper patina it had. Like all the cars before, he fueled it up at his own pump. That pump stood between the house and the barn—all three gone now, relegated to the dustbin of history—but one Sunday I stood right where the old pump stood, a yard from where Great-Uncle Searles tried to knife Dad one heated Sunday afternoon. You don't forget things like that.

As for Granddad's last car, the only places it went were pastures, Dad's saw shop and Price's Store, a classic country store with its roof now open to rain, soaking the very floors where Cokes bob in ice-filled vats in this boy's childhood memories. Granddad and Grandmom's house burned down. Someone tore down the old barn where a million fleas would hop on you, and Price's Store is mortally wounded. Damn if everything we love doesn't just rot away.

Some outbuildings are the only things left from my farm-exploring childhood. Granddad's dead. Grandmom's dead. (All my life I called her "Bama," the residue of childhood speech issues.) The homeplace burned.

Granddad Poland bounced his Chevy over many a terrace in the Double Branches community of Lincoln County, Georgia.

My childhood friends are grown and gone, and I have changed so much sometimes I don't even know who I am anymore. And Granddad's last car? Granddad died in 1972, and I figured I'd never see that car again, but I never forgot it. And then lo and behold, on February 18, 2018, when I was walking his old farm taking pictures and recalling things, I couldn't believe my eyes. There it was. His Bel Air was sleeping in a sepulcher of cedars and vines that had grown around it. Like a heart ripped from its body, the old battery sat on the ground still. Gave me a jolt.

I guess we've come full circle. Granddad used a car for a pickup. Back in the dark ages when I was in high school, you wouldn't be caught dead in a pickup. Uncool. Then the Ford Ranchero came along in 1957, and not to be outdone, Chevy's El Camino debuted in 1959. Things began to change.

Get feed and hay by weekday and go to church in your new pickup come Sundays, but pick up a date in one? No way. Well, the pickup ascended. There was a kid in my neighborhood who drove one. Thank goodness he's moved on. He souped it up and outfitted it with one of those annoying boombox systems you hear for miles. You know and I know he'd never drive it across a terrace in a pasture full of manure—sunbaked cakes as Mom referred to them. Cows would probably terrify him.

As for Granddad's cow-charming '65 Chevy, he probably got it from one of his favorite haunts, a junkyard. Over a handful of years, he made his last pasture rides in that car. And who went with him? I daresay none other than Roosevelt, staunch friend of the family. The times, something called change and a bad heart were about to leave Granddad in the dust. But his car is still with us. Joe Boy has left us, but it sits there waiting for Sweetie, Jabe and me. How I wish we could take another ride through Mr. Johnny's farm. We'd put a new battery in, get some tires and gas and head out. The things we'd talk about…riding through the pastures of long-lost youth and missing those white-faced cattle.

VANISHING SOUTHLAND

Much of what we saw during our drives has disappeared. Drive around and see for yourself. Here are sights nowhere as common as they once were.

JUNKYARDS

Sunday drives carried us past junkyards, past James Dickey's "parking lot of the dead" into no-man's land. There they were, wrecks by the score open to the sun and open to my little-boy eyes. Wrecks that scared me, that fascinated me with all their colors and randomly parked conveyances, parked seemingly forever. People died in some of the wreckage. Did I know any children left to grieve their parents, seemingly forever? No, but the day came when I knew a young girl whose grieving father planted a white cross in the ground.

Junkyards. So many cars, so many trucks, so much mangled steel. Junkyards scared me because of my first contact with a wreck. When I was seven, a speeding car lost control in a curve about a mile from home, killing a local girl. It so happens I rode the school bus with this dark-haired beauty. It so happens the wreck was in a friend's driveway. In a case of morbid curiosity, Dad drove me to the scene. People stood and stared. Shattered glass glittered and littered the road like sequins. The careening car had gashed open the ground, and car parts lay scattered like the bones of a luckless, long-gone dog. As everyone stared, I picked up a round black knob with one word in white set into it: "Heater." I slipped it into my pocket. Why? I still do not know.

Days later, the brutality that knob participated in got to me. I threw it as hard as I could into the pines, never to be seen again. Thus, did it escape the junkyard.

All these years later, I asked my friend Eddie Drinkard if he remembered the accident. I knew he would. "I will never forget it; may have blocked some of it out. It was at night but not late. I think her name was Lucinda Marie. The car was coming from your direction and hit the culvert at our driveway. I remember her brother coming. I took him into the house to use the phone. Not much talking between us. A few days later, her father put up a white wooden cross where my brother and I would wait for the bus. Don't think he ever quite got over it." I remember that cross. Each time the bus stopped at Eddie's, I stared at it. I know the car responsible for that cross must have ended up in a junkyard.

And then many years passed, and I began to see junkyards, iron bone yards of abandonment, as museums of sorts. Among the peeling paint, missing hoods and doors, cracked windshields, shattered headlights and strewn hubcaps, I'd spot old Fords and Chevys, chrome-shining beauties once upon a time turned queens, ravaged by time, gravity and sunlight. I'd spot a car with huge fins, a prehistoric shark sent to devour Volkswagen Beetles crushed at the intersection of bad luck and destiny. I spotted wrecks no mortal could live through, a junkyard's dark side.

For better or worse, junkyards became a necessity, and junkyards are where some ill-fated Sunday drives ended, but you can't see car morgues like you once did. Lady Bird Johnson's Highway Beautification Act required

that fence screens conceal junkyards. More than that, some simply vanished, relocated to parts unknown, but beauty is in the eye of the beholder, and I find strange beauty in the occasional multicolored crushed, twisted, smashed cars and trucks I stumble across. For one thing, they keep the past alive. Seeing the old Plymouths reminds me of Dad's devotion to Chrysler products and King Richard. I'm sure many a classic '57 Chevy has been cannibalized and reassembled as a restored beauty. And how many shade tree mechanics found cheap parts in the chain link kingdom where tires can't roll but dry rot instead? For many a fellow, a trip to a junkyard was mining for gold.

No, you just don't see junkyards like you used to. Back in the day, though, we'd pass an old junkyard and all heads would turn in its direction, drawn by some unknown force. No one said a word, but I know what we were thinking: "How many people died in all those rusting trucks and cars?" Blood and rust; they're a bit like twins, are they not? On we drove with many a question lingering in my mind. Junkyards. Strange places.

Years down the road now, from the comfort of my writing studio, I stretch my imagination, and up rises an image of junkyards as the old folks' home for cars and trucks. Their best days done, they find themselves heaped together in this final resting place, forced to be roommates. If each wreck could speak, it would recall its favorite trips, its favorite place to park, beneath a chinaberry perhaps, and the people it ferried across Mother Earth's face. Perhaps, too, it would reveal its fate: blown engine, head-on collision, obsolescence and a cancer called rust.

Dickey's "parking lot of the dead" was Steve Goodman's "graveyards of rusted automobiles" in "The City of New Orleans." As for me, all the colors, collisions and carnage make for a morgue of sorts, and I see a dark future some cannot avoid. A death synchronized with their car's demise. Others will ride off into the sunset like some scene from an old Western. Either way, all roads lead to junkyards. Just ask Janisse Ray. She knows that junkyards will never empty.

One of the "graveyards of the rusted automobiles," as Steve Goodman wrote in "The City of New Orleans."

MULES

Because of that lonely mule up on Highway 79, I came to exalt that legendary offspring of a female horse and donkey. The left-behind mule helped build the South and did so quietly without polluting the air. Then the combustion engine came along, and abandonment was the mule's fate. It had already been condemned to death in many a story, for it's been said no southern story is complete without a dead mule. Well, I suggest no southerner's childhood is complete lest mules plowed through it.

Down in Double Branches, that community of my father's people close by the Georgia–South Carolina border, I rode a mule on Granddad's farm. I rode it a lot, no saddle. My reward for riding that mule bareback was pain. That mule's sharp, bony vertebrae left soreness that lasted the rest of the day. Surely that mule had a name. I named it Stalwart for a while, as it deserved a name proper, but then my childhood friend Sweetie Boy (Jessie Lee Elam), who lived on Granddad's farm, told me the mule had a name: See It. Just like "see it," and often I saw See It but never knew its name.

Aside from me, See It had two burdens. It had a large, festering abscess on a knee. The second? Granddad had fastened a heavy chain to it. At the end of the chain was an old tire See It dragged around. I guessed that was to keep it from jumping fences, for we know bad things can happen when a mule gets into another farmer's pasture. Across the water in Edgefield in the 1940s, a mule kicked a calf in the head, killing it, and that led to murder for hire and eight people dead. Sweetie Boy said that wasn't the case, though. Granddad chained that tire to See It because the old fellow was too fast to catch.

I put the Edgefield story "How a Mule Kick Killed Eight People" in a book, my mule contribution to southern stories, but I assure you a distinguished list of writers ride on the ghosts of dead mules. Here come Truman Capote, William Faulkner, Erskine Caldwell, Richard Wright, Doris Betts, Reynolds Price, Clyde Edgerton, Larry Brown and Cormac McCarthy. So many writers have killed off mules that partly as parody and partly as scholarly research, Jerry Leath Mills, a University of North Carolina professor, dead like the mules he studied, developed a litmus test for what makes southern literature southern: "It has a dead mule in it."

Cormac McCarthy's *Blood Meridian* makes him the king of literary mule carnage. No fewer than 59 mules die in his book. Men shoot them, roast them, drown them and stab them, and mules die for want of water. In one scene, he does in 50 out of a *conducta* of 122 mules. They're packing in quicksilver for mining when an ambush runs them off a cliff. "The animals dropping silently as martyrs, turning sedately in the empty air and exploding on the rocks below in startling bursts of blood and silver as the flasks broke open and the mercury loomed wobbling in the air in great sheets and lobes and small trembling satellites. Half a hundred mules had been ridden off the escarpment."

In *Blood Meridian*'s alkali flats, dying of thirst becomes mules' fate where "black and desiccated shapes of horses and mules…parched beasts had died with their necks stretched in agony in the sand."

Mules and books don't always work out. Photographer Robert Clark and I put a barefoot, straw-hat farmer in a book, and it cost us. This farmer preferred to plow with a mule. Fender was his name. He had cut large holes in his hat so the mule could wear it, too. A government official considered buying one hundred copies of our book to recruit northern companies to South Carolina until he saw that barefoot farmer leaning against an old Ford V-8 pickup. "It depicts South Carolina as backwards," he declared. Never mind that mules built roads, bridges and railroads and cleared many a field. I'd like to have a dime for every mule that snaked logs out of woods.

This hardworking animal got the short end of the stick. We use mule similes and other figures of speech as insults. Dumb as a mule. Stubborn as a mule. Got beat like a rented mule. We even brand illegal drug couriers "mules." Rodney Dangerfield should have said, "I tell you, mules don't get no respect." Animal activists? Where were you when mules were work engines? Who speaks for our unremembered beast of burden? A legend, that's who.

We have to go out West to see a man defend a mule. In *A Fistful of Dollars*, Clint Eastwood, as "Joe," watches his mule panic and run off when banditos fire bullets around its hooves. Joe, clad in a serape, confronts the men to take up for his mule.

"You see, I understand you men were just playin' around, but the mule, he just doesn't get it. Course, if you were to all apologize…[The men laugh. Joe throws back his serape.] I don't think it's nice, you laughin'. You see, my mule don't like people laughin'. Gets the crazy idea you're laughin' at him. Now if you apologize, like I know you're going to, I might convince him that you really didn't mean it."

The laughing stops. The four banditos draw their guns, and Eastwood sends the foursome to eternity. Joe's mule gets the last laugh.

As for See It, my guess is Granddad had gotten him back during World War II. Mules can live well over twenty years, you know. Mules left farms about the same time draft mules left the army—replaced by the gasoline engine. Then World War II introduced gas rationing, and once again, farmers turned to their old friend for the war's duration. After some wartime plowing, retiree See It enjoyed life on the farm, except for that chain and tire. I have no idea what became of See It. Granddad's mule lies in an unmarked grave.

As I travel the back roads, I see donkeys and horses but few mules. They're fading from the southern landscape. 'Bout the only place they roam nowadays is books. You'll find 'em there, plowing the pages for eternity and doing what they do best.

Dying.

And in some cases receiving an honorable burial.

RIP FAITHFUL ONES: A POSTSCRIPT

Back in the 1940s, Sunday drivers up near Durham, North Carolina, driving a dirt road could see a mule cemetery on a ridge. I had to see this burial ground, and with the aid of my son-in-law's Garmin GPS, I found it, the resting place of mules and horses. To see this poignant cemetery is to see how urban encroachment chews up farmland. To see it is to witness a changing Southland. Granite tombstones stand in a ridge of woods overlooking I-540. To their back sits a large apartment complex. Farmland no more. Mules and horses no more. A man who loved and appreciated the hardworking animals that kept his farm and his life going buried them with dignity. Well, that was a ways back, before combustible engines put mules and horses out to pasture for good.

Mr. Fabius H. Page possibly is buried on this ridge as well. At least the coordinates for his grave will take you there. That's how we found the wooded graveyard for faithful farm animals. We parked and walked up a wooded ridge. Then we began to see the stones.

Lulu, Bay Mule, Very Swift, 1902,
Age 28

Bessie, Driving Mare, Brown, White Face, 4 White Feet, 1903–1937

You'll find eight other graves here, the resting place of Fab Page's beloved farm animals. Back then, locals knew the man who buried his animals with dignity as Fab. It's said that Fab's will stated that his family could not sell the land the cemetery is on. He intended it to be a perpetual memorial, and so far it is. It's not far from the Research Triangle Park. You can stand on this wooded ridge, close your eyes and imagine what Page's farm might have looked like. Perhaps a sweep of green pastures stood where the apartment complex and all its cars sit. Over there, perhaps, stood a handsome barn. As for I-540 with all its speeding traffic, we know this: it used to be a dirt road. Every Fourth of July, locals would host a horse race there. Now it's the site of traffic jams and accidents.

You can stand on that ridge with your eyes closed and imagine cattle lowing. You have to concentrate hard, however, to block out the commercial air flights roaring low overhead. You can imagine rows of corn standing green in the sun,

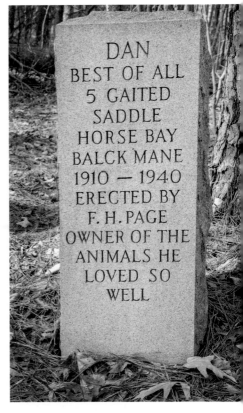

DAN
BEST OF ALL
5 GAITED
SADDLE
HORSE BAY
BALCK MANE
1910 — 1940
ERECTED BY
F. H. PAGE
OWNER OF THE
ANIMALS HE
LOVED SO
WELL

On a ridge of city-vanquished farmland near Durham, North Carolina, sits an old mule cemetery. RIP, faithful ones.

but that takes focus too. Asphalt and buildings dominate the land. Wholesale change has arrived full force.

A reporter for the *Athens Banner Herald*, Wayne Ford, wrote something I hold dear: "Tom Poland is an inquisitive man who keeps an eye out for extravagant chunks of nature, disappearing cultures, and people who are salt of the earth. Change is what Poland touches upon frequently." Indeed I do, and this mule and horse cemetery represents change in a way I have not seen. If you drive the land as much as I do, you will see junkyards filled with twisted, crushed, rusting vehicles. You will see, too, forsaken tractors overtaken by vines and weeds here and there. I suppose these are tractor cemeteries too, but I know of none with gravestones like those of Fab Page's mules and horses. The closest I have come to such a magnificent place is one granite tombstone for the grave of a dog.

I have no doubt these faithful beasts of burden were members of Fab Page's family, and it touches me that he erected monuments to them. I hope nothing ever disturbs this resting place. As much as anything, it is a memorial to a South the likes of which we will never see again. Each day, the ways of life and the land surrounding us die a little, and way too many fail to take notice.

Thank you, Fab Page. Long may your faithful ones rest in peace.

SMOKEHOUSES

Our Sunday drives often took me to my grandparents' home on the northern end of Lincoln County. They had a smokehouse, and from it "came the sweetest smoke a man was ever to smell." The late Harry Crews wrote that as he recalled his uncle Alton's smokehouse deep in South Georgia, down Bacon County way.

Granddad Walker's smokehouse sat just beyond his well next to a crabapple tree. It was dark, inside and out, and the fragrances seeping from it made you crave a ham biscuit. Shafts of light slanted from the roof, and motes of dust sparkled in beams of light. We kids didn't venture in there much. It was a bit foreboding, but what great meals came from it.

Memories of smokehouses connect me to simpler times. As I drive the back roads, I look for smokehouses. I've not seen many, and the most I see are in North Carolina around the Apex Durham region. Up there, new housing developments encroach onto farmland, but smokehouses have been spared here and there. And not just smokehouses but farm outbuildings. Not only do they add a quaint touch to the land, they remind us that people didn't always depend on grocery stores for their needs.

I have long been on the lookout for a smokehouse I could photograph up close. I found three. A fancy one sits along the South Carolina coast near Georgetown, the smokehouse at Hobcaw Barony where Bernard Baruch, advisor to seven presidents, lived. The second is the smokehouse at Chuck and Rose Lane Leavell's Charlane Plantation in Dry Branch, Georgia. The third is at Brattonsville in York County, South Carolina.

Hobcaw Barony in Georgetown, South Carolina. This smokehouse belonged to Bernard Baruch, the park bench statesman who advised U.S. presidents in two world wars.

Unlike Granddad's smokehouse, which sat on rocks, Baruch's sits on a brick foundation. The heavy door sits within stout framing. Cured hams represented a huge investment in money and labor, so smokehouse doors were strong, sturdy and locked to prevent thievery. Smokehouses were equivalent to today's refrigerators and freezers. You stored food for you, not thieves—nor invading troops.

Granddad Walker wrote a letter to the *Wilkes Reporter* many years ago. In that letter, he shared a smokehouse memory from the Civil War. Union forces were to come through his granddad's area. Knowing this, his granddad and some field hands took two dozen hogs from the smokehouse, leaving one ham in it. They went down to the creek and dammed it. Beneath the dam, they dug out the sand, hid the hogs and covered them with sand. They broke the dam and let the creek cover the hogs.

When Union soldiers went to raid his smokehouse, they saw that one ham in it. Said one soldier, "Leave it be. This poor devil just has one ham to make it through the winter with."

The smokehouse at Charlane Plantation belonged to Rose Lane Leavell's grandparents. When Rose Lane opened its red door, familiar scents poured out. You could still smell fragrant woodsmoke after all these years. Today, it's used for storage, but in the past, it was a savory source of cured meats, something her grandparents depended on.

The smokehouse at Brattonsville near McConnells, South Carolina, holds salted pork. Like all smokehouses, it has a dirt floor. Bacon and hams packed in salt looked as if snow had covered them. Ropes hung from beams, ready for hams. This smokehouse smelled as if was still in use, and in a way it is. Scenes for *The Patriot* were made here, and I don't know but maybe a Redcoat liberated a ham or two here.

Smokehouse memories...they belong to a class of memories that include country stores, outhouses and gristmills. So what happened to the old smokehouses of yesteryear? Most have been torn down by later generations who have no need to cure meat. A lot have succumbed to the elements. They went into the earth from whence they came. Some got in the way of progress when new home developments invaded the countryside. Thankfully, some smokehouses end up having their dense-grained longleaf pine salvaged by men like Edwin and Lowell Dowd, a father-son team in Prosperity, South Carolina. They own Dixie Heart Pine, and they will custom build you "furniture with a past and a future."

When someone tells them they have an old building with blackened wood, the Dowds know that beneath that weathered wood is red and yellow longleaf pine. The Dowds often make tables from such wood. So, wood that once cured hams can provide a setting for holiday dinners that feature ham and more. In a sense, these old smokehouses live on.

The smokehouse belonged to a time when people were far more self-sufficient. I'd like to think that a few will be preserved so the younger set and those yet to come can see how folks once lived. Granted, Mr. Baruch's smokehouse was fancy, but it did the same thing Granddad Walker's did: preserve meat and provide a sugary fragrance mixed with the smell of meat and smoke, "the sweetest smoke a man was ever to smell."

YARD ART

Remember these lines from an old Chuck Berry song? "Cruisin' and playin' the radio/With no particular place to go." Well, back in the day, we had no particular place to go, so we'd drive into the countryside come Sundays. It was there that we saw classic southern yard art. We'd see tree trunks painted white, swings suspended from big oak limbs, functional purple martin gourds and rows of tires half buried in the ground and painted white. Lawn jockeys, too.

Anyone who buys new tires today knows they have to pay a tire disposal fee. That wasn't a problem back in the day. Growing up, it was nothing to see truck tires made into flowerpots. Painted white and sheared to have scalloped edges, the pots held red geraniums. They were quite pretty and quite original.

Around the curve, rows of white-painted trees flanked a driveway, and up by a big old clapboard home, a homemade swing hung from a big oak. I'd see tires made into swings too. A tire swing is a scene right out of a Norman Rockwell painting.

People found new uses for old stuff before our throwaway society arrived. Giving junk a second life was alive and well back in the day, though it wasn't thought of as recycling. A nail-ruined tire could be turned into a flowerpot or swing. And some practicality backed some customs. Painting orchard trees white was considered a safeguard against fungi, disease and insects. I don't believe the painted trees I saw were being protected though. Who protects pines? No, I believe the folks who painted pine trunks white were simply trying to give their yards a more pleasing appearance.

Putting up purple martin gourds alleviated mosquito problems. When I see gourds dangling from a pole, I know I am deep into the country. Bottle trees have seen a bit of a revival. Today, people put them up because they see others put them up. Once the domain of the Lowcountry, you see bottle trees most anywhere. People in the Congo hung bottles from trees to ward off evil spirits, and slaves brought the practice here. Now they please the eye more than capture evil spirits as designed. Other oddities include miniature windmills and carved ducks with "windmill" arms that spin with the wind. For me, the true yard art of yesteryear is a row of half-buried tires edging a driveway. It steered you straight and most likely made finding the driveway at night a whole lot easier.

Over the years and miles, I've driven many a back road, and I have seen all kinds of yard art: miniature lighthouses; concrete "sculptures" of angels and cherubs; nonfunctioning fountains filled with flowers; and lawn jockeys, known as "Yardells. They have an origin in history, though it is viewed as doubtful. These statues, widely considered racially insensitive, supposedly symbolized a hero of African American history and culture. The River Road African American Museum in Donaldsonville, Louisiana, says the lawn jockey has its roots in one Jocko Graves, an African American youth who served with General George Washington. When Washington crossed the Delaware to ambush British forces, he considered Graves too young for such danger and left him behind to tend to the horses and keep a light on the bank for their return.

Jocko Graves, faithful to his post and orders, froze to death during the night, the lantern still in his hand. The young fellow's devotion so moved Washington that he had a statue sculpted of him holding the lantern. Washington installed the statue at his Mount Vernon estate, referring to it as *The Faithful Groomsman*. True? Who knows, but true or not, lawn jockeys were a fixture in yards and along driveways. Today, most are hidden away or repainted white.

Sunday drives served up quirky, interesting sights: old claw-foot tubs filled with flowers, totem poles carved from trees and more. Now we live in times when most people are content with yards free of art, outside of seasonal flags, bottle trees and reflecting balls. I saw a lady's home once where she had turned her ex-husband's bowling ball into what appeared to be a reflecting ball. Bury tires halfway along your driveway and the homeowners' association will come knocking. Truth be told, that old custom probably needed to go.

One Sunday, hit a back road and see what you can find as yard art from yesteryear goes. Take the lesser-traveled roads, the kinds that lead to old stores and nonincorporated communities. Should you find an old tar-and-gravel or, even better, dirt road, take it and travel back in time. Take photos, because you'll not see the likes of some things again.

GAS STATION BISCUITS

Our Sunday drives never took us by fast-food restaurants; there were none. What a blessing that was. We'd see small concrete block hamburger joints, and gas stations sometimes offered something hot to eat. The food was always good. Well, a few gas stations still cook food for folks weary of fast food. My being from Georgia and a fan of back roads and small towns prompted my North Carolina friend Martha to mail me a clipping from *Bon Appétit* magazine, "The Best Biscuits in Georgia." The story's about a Chevron station in Between, Georgia. The name fits. Between is betwixt Athens and Atlanta.

The story related how Felicia Doster arrives at 4:30 in the morning to make biscuits from scratch and hand rolls 'em for regulars and others sure to come. By the time her day ends, she's made and served some three hundred biscuits—plain, sausage, bacon, egg and cheese. After reading about Biscuit Queen Felicia Doster, I recalled gas stations I've seen converted to restaurants.

On Highway 176, a far better route to Charleston than crowded I-26, I stopped in Cameron at a gas station that serves some pretty good hot dogs. One summer, I had some barbecue on St. Simon's Island at an old gas station turned restaurant. From gas station to gastronomical, they're out there: service stations turned cafés, restaurants and pubs. For a while, the folks in my hometown had an old filling station, as we call them, that had been converted to a restaurant, Soap Creek Restaurant. It's a Mexican restaurant now. I sit there in that old station trying to imagine cars on a rack getting an oil change and tires changed.

In *South Carolina Country Roads*, I wrote about Harold's Country Club down Yemassee way. You'll find it off Highway 21 at 97 Highway, 17A. What would become Harold's Country Club began in the 1930s as a Chevrolet dealership. Harold Peeples bought what had become an old-fashioned garage and gas station in 1973. In the late 1970s, friends and neighbors began a beautiful custom: gathering for covered dish suppers on Thursday nights. Over time, the group began cooking and eating in the garage to avoid bad weather and the gnats and mosquitoes for which the Lowcountry is famed. As Thursday evening gatherings grew, Harold took over the cooking, charging a small amount to cover expenses. In time, Friday wings and things and Saturday steaks joined the menu. Today, it's a popular, legendary restaurant.

All over the South, people are converting all sorts of buildings into restaurants. One summer day, I met my sisters at an old country store/old post office turned restaurant up near Belton, South Carolina, Grits & Groceries. It's worth the drive. The food is fabulous.

I see wreckage along the back roads, and a lot of times that wreckage includes an old service station that has given up the ghost. Take Burckhalter's on Highway 28 south of McCormick, South Carolina. What if some entrepreneur came along and turned Burckhalter's into a restaurant? It has ample parking space. Someone could tear up the inside and retrofit it into a modern restaurant. Do what needs to be done to meet health and legal requirements. Conjure up a theme and some supporting art and interior design.

Envision a beautiful awning over that dented metal door, replaced by a beautiful wood and glass door. Knock out some blocks and put in windows. Get rid of that dark garage door and make that bay into a dining area and create a dining area in an open-air setting. Throw in some bright-red umbrellas over white tables and add some potted flowers and landscaping. Put up a beautiful fountain, four tiers. A new coat of paint and some nice lighting fixtures sound good too. How about some beautiful wood flooring.

Resurface that old parking lot and add some bright white strips to the black asphalt. Give the place a unique name and some cool signage. Maybe stick with its history. "Drive Up, Fill Up" might do. Hire and train the staff. All-important are the menu and hours. Get all that settled and do a little advertising. Now it's time for the grand opening.

Dream on, you're saying, and you're probably right. All that takes a lot of money, and besides, they tore down Burckhalter's. It is no more, but as I drive the back roads, I see a lot of places that were converted into restaurants, and guess what? They're closed. The ones that make it, however, do well. People along the back roads appreciate good places to eat, and they spread the word when the food is good. As fellow writer Aida Rogers advises, "Stop where the parking lot is full."

In the feature about Felicia Doster's biscuit business, there's a telling quote near the end. Brandon Chonko, a chicken and hog farmer, told writer Wyatt Williams, "South Georgia would starve without gas stations." Williams went on to write, "In Reidsville, near his [Chonko's] farm, every single gas station has a biscuit. After all, what's the point of stopping for gas if you can't fill up too?"

I agree. Give me a converted filling station over a bland fast-food franchise where you take a number to be served and make your own drink. Give me a back-road dive where fan belts hang on the wall and two pumps serve gas out front. Give me a place with character. Give me a place where long ago, a country proprietor wrote out receipts on a pad. And give me one more thing: homemade biscuits when dew's on the grass and I stop to fill up, not the car, but myself.

MOM-AND-POP DRIVE-INS

Many a Sunday drive ended with a treat. Mom and Dad would take us on a countryside jaunt, often into South Carolina, and that generally meant a return trip on Highway 378. During the early 1960s, we'd pull up to the 378 Drive-In, operated by a fellow by the name of Voyles. Clarence Voyles. It consisted of a hardwood floor, counter, booths and a jukebox where 45 RPMs played the hits of the '60s. There may have been a pinball machine, too. For sure there was one of those bowling games where you slid a heavy metal disc over finely powdered sawdust toward pins hanging from a wildly lit platform. Bowl a strike and all the pins disappeared to a clatter of metal. Bowl too hard and the metal disc would bounce back. In a carryover from the late '50s, girls wore bobby socks and saddle shoes. Boys in muscle cars circled the drive-in in endless orbits of gas-guzzling, growling engines.

We stayed in the car to be served. The fare consisted of burgers and Cokes and French fries and a great hamburger steak. High school classmate Janis Hawes Reynolds remembers the food: "As you neared the old 378 Hamburger Drive-In, you could smell those burgers and fries cooking. You'd start salivating. The bright lights would just make you feel happy."

Garnett Wallace remembers that the 378 Drive-In served supper to the football teams before home games. A hamburger steak dinner was $1.25, and it was a great place to hang out on Friday and Saturday nights. "We would drive around it every so often to see who was there. Gene Frazier worked as a 'hop' for a while, as did many others," he said.

My chief memories of the place involve the cars that revved their engines outside cruising 'round and 'round the place, crunching gravel.

Back then, a few fellows sported ducktail haircuts doomed to surrender to Beatle hairstyles. Ducktail dudes' muscle cars were part of the classic car era. Back then, the bigger and faster a car was, the better. Among their ranks were the Pontiac GTO coupe and the Chevrolet Chevelle. I recall a few Corvettes, Dodge Chargers and Thunderbirds. Other cars of the era were the Plymouth Road Runner and the Chevy Camaro Super Sport. These cars were simply small cars with big engines, meant for street racing and dragging. As well, there were some classic 1957 Chevys with roll and pleated seats. I recall that Gartrell Blackman had a '57 Chevy that was the envy of all. Some cars looked like strange fish.

Remember cars with big fins? Inspiration came from a World War II fighter aircraft, Lockheed's twin-tailed P-38 Lightning. A car designer gave the 1948 Cadillac fins, paying homage to that legendary fighter plane. Soon, other car designers copied that Cadillac's style. The late 1950s gave us extreme fins, and these ridiculous fins eventually shamed car designers into scaling them way back.

1961. The era of big fins died. And so did a way of life. A lot of change was about to unfold. Men wore crew cuts, and women wore bouffant hairstyles. Alan Shepard became the first American to go into space. Ernest Evans, a kid from Spring Gulley, South Carolina, started a dance craze with a song. You know him as Chubby Checker, and the song was "The Twist."

I remember riding into town with Dad in his 1961 big-finned white Chrysler Newport with pale blue interior. Viewed from the side, his car looked like a paper airplane, sleek and aerodynamic. Saturdays in that dart-like car we'd fetch barbecue in downtown Lincolnton. Another drive-in, the Milky Way Freeze Bar, run by Mrs. Suzie Power, was a favorite hangout on Sunday evenings. You'd order at one window, I believe, and pick up your food at another window. I've been to many a hamburger joint in my time, but none smelled as good or had burgers as good as the old Milky Way Freeze Bar.

In the summer, we all hung out at the park and its concession stand on the hill overlooking the swimming area. The hamburgers there were good also, and seems there was a record player of some type there as well.

All these memories come to me in fits and starts, and I'm sure many of you better recall those days when life seemed simpler and in many ways a lot better than today despite the so-called progress we've seen. Every generation has its hangouts, and for many of us baby boomers, life in the 1960s meant evenings at the drive-in and hamburger joints. Whenever I pass these spots, my mind drifts back to the 1960s. That was our era and those were our places. It was all we had, and it was more than enough.

FAMILY REUNIONS

There were Sunday drives when we'd drive by big family gatherings. By a church, in a green field, beneath big shade trees, everyone seemed to be having fun. Even better, there were Sunday drives when we had a specific destination: family, fun and good food, all wrapped up in a tradition called "family reunion." I clearly recall family reunions with my mother's people. All the kids would play while adults caught up and prepared the food. At one such gathering, an elderly fellow cut a stalk of sugar cane and gave pieces of it to the kids.

Each summer, cutting stalks of sugar cane and sucking the sweetness was popular at that reunion, as was winding up an old wooden bucket from the well and drinking water with a bite of cold in it. Investigating the smokehouse was fun, as was eating crabapples and harassing girls who dared to use the outhouse. Yes, in the 1950s and 1960s, a family reunion was a big thing.

It's not a big thing today. Stores are open Sundays, and people have all kinds of ways to visit without meeting face to face thanks to technology. Back in the day, however, many a Sunday drive took us past an old homeplace where folks milled about and kids ran to and fro. A reunion was underway. The aroma of fried chicken, potato salad and more filled the air.

These days, I don't have much hope for cousins getting to know one another. Considering just how scattered families are today, you'd think the family reunion would be more important than ever. It isn't, but some determined people carry on that fine tradition. On the second Sunday in September, aircraft of various vintages invade northern Lincoln County,

Georgia. There's a unique story behind this friendly invasion. It began as a birthday party that turned into a family reunion. How did that happen? History holds the answer.

In the early part of the last century, the Rhodes family, a hardworking farm family, lived in northern Lincoln County beyond Pistol Creek. When World War II swept through the world, military aircraft often flew over their farm. Bobby, the son of John and Eula Rhodes, would stop chopping cotton to watch the planes, and dreams of flying filled his head. Even today, you can hear the excitement in his voice. "I even saw one of the planes fly over that bombed and jammed the rudder on the German battleship *Bismarck*," said Bobby. "When I saw a zeppelin, that set me on fire."

Bobby taught himself to fly those many years ago when times were simpler, before red tape and regulations complicated men's ambitions. Bobby's brother Claude learned to fly also. But that was worlds ago. Claude has passed away and the cotton fields are long gone but a unique reunion carries on. It's a good story that takes place in an area steeped in legend.

You can trace the fly-in's origin to a one-hundred-year-old tenant shack. In this picturesque cabin, boys destined to become pilots were born in a historic locale. Just three miles away, near the Chennault place, someone robbed the Confederate gold train, an event shrouded in mystery ever since. Naturalist William Bartram, whose *Travels in Georgia and Florida* is a classic of American natural history, explored the area in 1773. Clarks Hill Lake, backed up from the Savannah, lies within walking distance of the Rhodes homeplace. The edge of the lake turns up Indian artifacts, and it's not unusual to see an osprey share the sky with the airplanes. Nearby is an old slave cemetery. The setting is rich in history: man's, nature's and a family's.

The Rhodes reunion is a story of family, good southern food and togetherness. It actually began as a birthday party for the Rhodes brothers' mom, Eula Rhodes (Granny), and continued until she died at the age of ninety-nine. After Granny died, no birthday party took place for two years, but everyone missed seeing each other so much that the boys resurrected the birthday party as a reunion on Granny's birthday. Bobby led the initial effort, and in time, the young guys stepped up to give the old guard a rest. An event this big requires a lot of planning and work. For one thing, the 2,700-foot runway needs mowing. Doug, Phillip, Michael and Kelvin—sons of deceased brother Presley—pitch in, as do Eddie and Wade, Claude's sons, and Chris, Bobby's son. Now, on the second Sunday in September, descendants of John Morgan Rhodes and Lois (Wright) Rhodes gather at John Wright and Eula Lee (Walker) Rhodes's old homestead for a reunion.

The birthday-party-turned-reunion takes place amidst a curious mix of the old, modern and remote. To start, the setting brings to mind a far-flung outpost in the Australian Outback. You won't see power lines, which is good for the pilots. Man-made power consists of nothing but an old windmill that has seen better days. Only the water tank remains, perched on a tower bereft of its blades and tail. Running west to east, just behind the old homeplace, the grass runway rolls across the land, making it easy to imagine a bush pilot coming in laden with supplies for an isolated outpost.

The runway makes this a reunion like no other. Years back, the Rhodes boys began inviting a few pilot friends, and the flying fraternity spread the word. The birthday party evolved into a "fly-in" where pilots from all walks of life flew in for good food, good times and good people. Now a lot of folks come to see the planes land and depart.

Attending the fly-in gives one a feeling akin to a festival, political stump and football game. Chords of bluegrass rise above the murmur of people and hum of generators. Children jump and slide on air-inflated bounce houses. People lie on blankets by the runway, watching planes come and go. Large smoking grills fill the air with the aroma of six hundred pounds of Boston butts, and nearby a kettle of hash big enough for *Macbeth*'s three witches simmers. RVs and campers provide overnight accommodations, like at a football game.

All this takes place around the old homeplace, which Bobby's granddad built more than 110 years ago. Its ancient pine boards were milled at an old mill in Grovetown owned by Paul Corley, the first man to put a DC electric motor on a golf cart, a latter-day version of which roams the grounds. A large shed accommodates the hundreds who come to reestablish ties, catch up, enjoy the good southern cuisine and watch the planes come and go. Claude Rhodes, who died eight years ago, designed the large shed, beneath which tables twenty yards long sag with great heaps of food. While the men oversee the barbecuing of pork, the women lay out pies, cakes, potato salad, fried chicken, medleys of vegetables and other fixings. Girls beneath a tent stay busy setting out iced tea and other beverages.

Between the old home and shed, a massive live oak Bobby's mother planted some eighty-five years ago provides shelter from the sizzling September sun. One year, Augusta mayor Deke Copenhaver gave grace beneath the large oak, standing on a metal bench that was once part of a prison. Besides family members, area ministers, politicians and musicians, many interesting personages come, but the pilots provide the excitement.

On the second Sunday in September, airplanes descend onto a grassy 2,700-foot runway in Lincoln County, Georgia, for the fly-in family reunion.

As people meander and reconnect, the pilots fly in and out, in effect putting on an informal air show. A daunting touch-and-go now and then turns heads. A friend of Bobby's, a famous ace from the Korean War—the late Phil Colman—a double ace with ten kills to his credit, some in China, attended the reunion. Only a handful of documented double aces exist since the United States formed aviation combat units. Acclaimed author James Salter, who flew missions with Colman, immortalized him in *Burning the Days* for his crash landing of an F-86, wheels up, on railroad tracks in Korea. Other noted pilots come, such as Joe Miles, a member of the P-51 Mustang Pilots Association, and Wayne Van Valkenburgh, a retired Eastern Airlines pilot from Warren, Arkansas.

A U.S. flag serves as an air sock for the pilots streaming in over the treetops. Many pilots come from a grass airstrip just off Deans Bridge Road in Blythe, Georgia, affectionately referred to as the "Pea Patch." Airplanes from Stapelton and Louisville, Georgia, fly in, as do ultralights from Trenton, South Carolina. Noting the ultralights lined up prettily one September

Sunday, Bo Rhodes, who lives nearby, nodded and said, "I thought I heard a swarm of ultralights come in this morning."

A Beechcraft Bonanza drops from the sky, touches and goes. Local pilot Gary Ward comes back around and lands. Planes are everywhere: lined up along the side of the runway, in the air, landing and taking off. Colorful and sleek, they command the eye. A lemon-and-white Citabria owned by Edwin Brock of Melrose, Florida, is a striking craft, a two-seater designed for flight training and personal use. It's capable of sustaining aerobatic stresses, as its name, "airbatic," spelled backward, reflects. The planes possess names as interesting as the men who love them: a Rans Airaile S12, a Challenger Two, an N3 Pup, a Cessna 172, a Piper Cub Tri Pacer and a small canvas-covered plane with the misleading words "US Army Sky Raider" embellishing it.

One plane in particular deserves mention: a 1946 vintage Taylorcraft, legendary among pilots for its abilities. On its tail is a tagline that's much more than marketing hype: "Built to Fly." The Taylorcraft was Bobby Rhodes's first plane. Bobby soloed at twenty-two and flew it for ten years. As time passed, the man and the plane parted. Then a friend and relative tracked the plane down, finding it in North Carolina. That very same Taylorcraft is still flying, and now it's part of the fly-in.

Food, flying, family, fun and friends. That's the fly-in. Bluegrass on Saturday night and the main event on Sunday. It makes for a great weekend of food, family and memories that Granny would certainly appreciate. As much as anything though, it provides a glimpse back to a more innocent time when men from the greatest generation could teach themselves to fly, something impossible in the regulated world of today. And it gives us a glimpse, too, of a time when a Sunday drive sometimes led to a family reunion.

OLD BRIDGES

Sundays we would occasionally cross steel truss bridges. As you drove over them, they made a noise—a metallic *whoosh*. Today, old steel truss bridges are relegated to back roads, but that's what we traveled many a Sunday. Going, going, gone are the old rusty steel truss bridges. Today we have wide concrete bridges. The old bridges? Many have been removed, but if you know where to go, you can find old bridges, and when you do, see if you don't find them elegantly beautiful.

Old bridges from our Sunday drive days still stand. Ghostly, overtaken by woods and vines, they stand alone. No traffic crosses them now. The beauty of old bridges should not be lost so easily. You can catch glimpses of them. Driving Highway 378 from Saluda to McCormick, look to your right as you cross Hard Labor Creek. Through the trees, an old bridge materializes. I parked and visited it one afternoon. Surreal but real, it hosted a deer hunter's hut-like stand in its middle, right where old cars and trucks once sped. Hard Labor Creek runs on as if nothing has changed, but it has.

If you take Highway 283 out of Plum Branch toward Edgefield, you'll see Key Road to your right. Take it and you will cross where an old steel truss bridge once stood over Stevens Creek. Just past its site is a turn off to the right that takes you to another old bridge. Here you can walk out on yet another steel truss bridge and see the Key Road Bridge. Two old steel bridges side by side—twins, for a while. One was for cars, and one's for couples, bikers and hikers. At one end of the "walking" bridge is Edgefield

Watson Mill Covered Bridge, Georgia's longest, spans 229 feet across the South Fork River. Covering wooden bridges strengthened and protected them.

County; at the other, McCormick County. The view provides one of those scenes Hollywood would love for one of its old movies.

Yes, old bridges are still with us but on life support. When I see a forsaken bridge clinging to life, I conjure up images of classic old cars and trucks. Think about the people, long gone, who depended on those bridges to get from one place to another.

Here's another old one. Highway 181 crosses a free-running stretch of the Savannah River just below Lake Hartwell. You can see this old steel truss bridge jutting just over the state line into South Carolina. The authorities spared it. As I wrote in my back roads book *South Carolina Country Roads*, "Neither you nor I will ever cross that bridge again. Its South Carolina terminus has been cut away. It hangs over the river, a dropping off point if ever there were one. A wide concrete bridge, which seems to be the trend, now, has replaced it. Barriers prevent you from driving onto the old bridge. Drive across this bridge and you essentially walk the plank with a plunge into the Savannah River your fate." Beside it runs the new span that, quite simply, lacks character. Think of a parking lot hung over a river.

We lost our covered bridges long ago. Now we're losing the old steel truss bridges. Sure, they are narrow and creaky, but they're also beautiful.

Located near Comer, Georgia, and not far from the South Carolina state line, the covered Watson Mill Bridge pulls people back again and again. It makes for a fine Sunday drive, but it's more than that—it's a drive into a bygone era when men covered bridges to protect their structural timbers. In the act of doing so, they gave us a rare form of architectural beauty. A wooden bridge complete with cover, all held together by wooden pins—a rarity in this era of steel and cement bridges.

Washington W. King, son of freed slave and well-known covered bridge builder Horace King, built the 229-foot bridge in 1885. It replaced an earlier structure that Gabriel Watson, owner of the original mill here, built near the site of the present bridge. A rising south fork of the Broad River washed the old bridge away.

An early owner of the Watson Mill land put up a hydroelectric plant that generated energy from the south fork of the Broad River. That power ran a mill complex, blacksmith shop, store and hotel. Rural electrification brought an end to the generation of power there.

You could drive the state of Georgia entire, but you'd never find a longer covered bridge than this one with its truss town lattice. In fact, it ranks among the country's longest covered bridges.

People drive to Watson Mill Bridge State Park to enjoy the peaceful setting. The bridge and Broad River's white water create a scene akin to an extraordinary setting in a movie.

Folks along the Georgia–South Carolina border can make a Sunday drive to this beautiful setting and recapture a past when people clad in old-timey bathing suits slid on the Broad River's slippery rocks. To see the bridge is to see the past, when roads were narrow and times simpler.

A FINE OLD INN

Fast-food franchises serve monotony along highways. In earlier times, folks packed picnic-style lunches for roadside dining. Home cookin' can't be beat. As I wrote in "Burma-Shave," Mom would fry chicken and bake a ham for long treks. We really did eat like kings.

Today, short trip or long, a boring franchise restaurant ruins the joy of dining on the road. Plastic packets of condiments. A profusion of paper, cardboard, Styrofoam, paper cups—it's maddening. There's a place on the South Carolina coast, however, where you can experience the simplicity of yesteryear and class at the same time. Return to the days of glassware, china and silverware.

At Pawleys Island, you can step into an inn that will take you back to the days before air conditioning, credit cards and predictable menus rendered road meals a chore and a bore. This fine old inn requires reservations, and no, it does not accept credit cards. Nor do you sit and order from a menu. You eat what's planned for the day, and you do so with relish. Tuesday is fried chicken day.

Sea View Inn is a breath of fresh air. No, more precisely, it's a refreshing sea breeze, commanding a front-row view of the Atlantic as it does. Out front is a porch with rockers and a joggling board. A library-like sitting room and a sunroom offer relaxing accommodations. As lunch or dinnertime nears, people walk up the boardwalk out back to the double screen doors at the back of the inn. Inside, they engage in friendly talk until the bell summons diners. Look for the table with a white envelope with your name on

With an ocean breeze on one side and a marsh on the other, dine as folks did before air conditioning arrived.

it. Treasure the balmy sea breezes sifting through screen windows. The white smock–clad staff provides expert service with smiles and true friendliness as it delivers the food. Note the rivulets of condensation trickling down your glass of iced tea. Note the wicker baskets of biscuits. Pats of real butter—not some soft yellow concoction in a plastic condiment package.

The clinking of china, the ringing of silverware and pleasant undertones of conversation make for a charming medley. Through the front windows, the rockers sit empty. People are dining as the Atlantic crests and falls, as it has for eons. It's dinnertime at the Sea View Inn, and you are there.

Put your cash and tip in the plain white envelope. No fussy credit card transactions—no swiping and no identity theft with cash.

No fast food here. You must make your reservation days in advance, so you can see that to dine here is to retreat to some golden age lost beneath a crush of wheels pounding an interstate. No one-word name signifying fast food, no Hardees, Zaxby's, McDonald's, Sonic or Applebee's even. Three words: Sea View Inn, and you do, indeed, view the sea, not some busy street or an endless parking lot known as an interstate. Thank heavens for the Sea View Inn and its enduring presence.

For more than eighty years, the Sea View Inn has welcomed guests to its seashore setting. It proudly proclaims that it's "the only beachfront dining on Pawleys." Built in 1937, the Sea View Inn features fourteen rooms in the main house and six rooms in the adjacent cottage. Many guests return year after year to vacation with their families. They make "extended family" from friendly guests who share the same week or weekend. All appreciate the return to the charm, old-fashioned fabulous service and Lowcountry cuisine. Here you can escape the franchises and enjoy wonderful meals three fabulous times each day. Just listen for the bell for the 8:30 breakfast, 1:15 midday meal and 6:15 supper. Yes, I said supper.

MEMORY LANE

Our Sunday drives amounted to a trip down a memory lane in the making tour, for much of what we saw in the 1950s, '60s and early '70s would vanish. Bidding adieu they were back then, only we didn't know it. In the years to come, many small farms would disappear, replaced by housing developments or absorbed into corporate farms. Self-made toys would disappear, replaced by cheap, mass-produced plastic playthings. Places that used to lure tourists, well, they faded too, literally in some cases. When's the last time you saw a See Rock City barn?

And ways of life would die off. Remember handheld funeral home fans? And how about screen wire fly swatters? Many of us had grandmothers who grew old-timey petunias. You'll be hard-pressed to see those today. A farmer plowing a field with a mule? A woman sprinkling clothes to be ironed with an old Coca-Cola bottle? How about a sawdust pile, once a source of fun for daring kids and mulch for gardeners? Quaint steel truss bridges?

When I recall the Sunday drives our family made, I'm recalling things you don't see much of nowadays.

BURMA-SHAVE

When I was a boy, family trips to Florida felt like one big Sunday drive, and each Sunday drive felt like going on vacation. Drives back then were fun. We were young and naïve, and looking back, that was a good thing. We didn't have a way to tell everybody every little thing we were doing. We pretty much lived in isolation, so when we ventured into the world, it was cause for excitement. Every Sunday drive was a bit like a vacation. It was a feeling I never lost.

***

In the late 1950s and early 1960s, we traveled a lovely seaside lane, a highway with an alphanumeric poetic name: A1A, known also as the Indian River Lagoon Highway. What a magical route. It's been said no stretch of highway reaches further into America's history than A1A. It reaches back into my memory as well. In the 1950s, we set our sights on that highway, and near Amelia Island, state road A1A waited.

Along its route, we encountered odd little red-and-white road signs: America's oldest city, St. Augustine and its old fort, an alligator farm and more. The main thing we kids longed for, of course, was the ocean. When you grow up landlocked, every time you see the ocean it's like the first time you saw it. Nothing beats the sight of the sprawling Atlantic.

What we couldn't know back then was that we were trendsetters. My family took part in the early years of vacationing when it was not yet a full-blown tradition. Taking a summer vacation began not long after World War II ended. Several things seared the summer vacation into Americans' consciousness. Servicemen returning from the war began to marry, and couples had babies—baby boomers. Postwar prosperity gave families extra money to spend on shiny new cars. The automobile gave people a way to make road trips and Sunday drives. After years of doing without thanks to the Depression and World War II, families hit the road in the 1940s and 1950s.

Cheaper than cheap, gas was not an issue. Dad drove us to Florida in his 1956 chrome-trimmed Plymouth Belvedere. We would leave in predawn darkness to avoid as much heat as we could. As the day warmed up, driving through tar puddles sounded like duct tape being ripped up. Sectioned concrete highways gave travel a rhythm. We'd spot a dead armadillo in the road with great excitement, a sign we were in Florida. The trip gave me memories of two icons: A1A, Florida's beautiful seaside highway, and those odd little rhyming road signs promoting a brushless shaving cream, Burma-Shave.

Does Your Husband Misbehave, Grunt and Grumble, Rant and Rave,
Shoot the Brute Some Burma-Shave.

A1A was like no other highway I'd seen, a seashore version of the Blue Ridge Parkway. A1A flirted with the Atlantic, winding through lush tropical vegetation and serving up beautiful ocean vistas.

A deep history runs along A1A, all of which escaped me back then. During the Civil War, Confederates used beach areas there as a salt works. The Southern boys extracted salt from seawater and cured beef jerky from cattle raised in Florida. They shipped the jerky north to feed Confederate troops.

The only salt that concerned me was the Morton Salt on the tomato sandwiches Mom had packed and the salt that would cling to my skin after long swims in the Atlantic Ocean. Fast-food joints had yet to blight the land, and we packed our own picnic-style lunches. Mom would fry chicken and bake a ham for the journey. We took watermelons too. We ate like kings.

She Put a Bullet Through His Hat,
But He's Had Closer Shaves Than That, With Burma-Shave

We often stopped at a park in Swainsboro, Georgia, as we worked our way south. Elsewhere, we'd look for a good place to pull over and eat home-cooked food. It was better eating and better for us. Progress isn't always progress. We looked with great excitement to the fresh seafood we'd get in Florida.

The Monkey Took One Look at Jim, and Threw the Peanuts, Back at Him, He Needed Burma-Shave

We'd stay in concrete block motels with crank-out windows. Utilitarian with no frills, they served their purpose: a place to sleep. Come morning, we set out exploring. We toured the old Spanish fort in St. Augustine, known today as Castillo de San Marcos National Monument. The fort, built from coquina—small seashells naturally bonded together—was soft but durable. I loved walking its large square and checking out its garrisons.

Between St. Augustine and Ormond Beach sat an iconic place, Marineland. It was a big part of the trip. Going to breakfast at Marineland's Dolphin Restaurant was unforgettable. Outside stood a large three-dimensional dolphin. Inside, glasses of fresh-squeezed orange juice waited on crisp, white linen tablecloths. After breakfast, we'd watch porpoises perform tricks.

Dinah Doesn't Treat Him Right, But If He'd Shave, Dyna-Mite! Burma-Shave

Another great stop along A1A was the alligator farm. The St. Augustine Alligator Farm Zoological Park began in the late nineteenth century as a small exhibition of Florida reptiles and became a quintessential Florida attraction. We had to see it. Ostriches, crocodiles, Galapagos tortoises, monkeys, birds and many examples of Florida's native wildlife were there. As we watched men rope and wrestle big gators, Mom went into its gift shop and looked over pottery the Cash family hand-painted.

If the journey was part of our destination, then the red-and-white Burma-Shave signs surely made the trip more entertaining. These signs with their offbeat humor were as much a part of the trip as stopping for gas. Not long after our Florida trips in the late 1950s, change began to work against the little signs. Faster cars rolling down superhighways led to the monstrous, unsightly billboards we're cursed with today.

The Big Blue Tube's, Just Like Louise, You Get a Thrill, from Every Squeeze, Burma-Shave

We made good family trips back then. We saw new sights and built great memories. We ate well. We didn't rush in and out of fast-food joints. We didn't buzz through drive-through windows. We picnicked at roadside parks.

I don't recall that Dad drove fast, but Burma-Shave had a sign for those who did:

Slow Down, Pa, Sakes Alive, Ma Missed Signs Four and Five, Burma-Shave

Burma-Shave gave other highways an aura, but A1A, the road to Burma-Shave, forever gave me that Sunday drive feeling when we set out on adventure all those years ago.

SEE ROCK CITY

n Mom's backyard, an old red-and-black birdhouse sits high on a white pole. It's a small-scale barn, and painted on its roof are iconic words: "See Rock City." Times were, you could drive along a back road, and sooner or later you'd see a barn with its roof turned into an advertisement. Those iconic messages worked. We went to see Rock City.

Today, it's not as easy to come across a barn roof declaring "See 7 States from Rock City." In case you've never heard of it, Rock City is a roadside attraction in Lookout Mountain, Georgia. Huge rock formations, a Lovers Leap and caverns with black lights, I recall. I remember, too, Ruby Falls, but that's an attraction inside Lookout Mountain.

I saw Rock City as a boy. The barn you see here stands on Highway 28 between McCormick and Abbeville. All these years it was close by. Weathered with boards missing and gaping holes, the old barn stands as a museum, a survivor, South Carolina's sole Rock City barn.

A fellow by the name of Clark Byers climbed on top of that barn. Byers's barn-painting career started in 1935 when Rock City founder Garnet Carter turned country barns into Rock City billboards. He found a receptive audience in Depression-weary Americans who were ready to travel and see the land. An ad on a barn's rooftop had to provoke curiosity.

Carter's public attraction, Rock City, officially opened on May 21, 1932. Soon after, Carter enlisted the help of a young sign painter from Trenton, Georgia. He hired Clark Byers to travel highways and paint three simple words on barns: "See Rock City." Byers painted the words freehand, and the size of the barn determined the message. The bigger the barn, the bigger the message. The distinctive black-and-white signs appeared as far north as Michigan and as far west as Texas. Rock City gave the farmers three dollars or free passes to Rock City and, in some cases, Rock City thermometers and bathmats in exchange for turning their barn roofs into ads.

Before painting barns, Byers worked in a cotton mill and bottled buttermilk for three dollars a week. He would go on to paint barns for three decades, dodging bulls, clinging to slippery roofs and scanning the horizon for thunderstorms. He retired in 1969 after nearly being electrocuted by lightning while repainting a barn. He had painted approximately nine hundred barns in nineteen states. Byers died in 2004. He was eighty-nine.

Weather and time and something ironic robbed us of Byers's work. Many vintage Rock City barns suffered a needless fate thanks to the scourge known as politicians. If they're not renaming lakes, putting their names on highways and in general throwing history into the trash can, politicians find ways to destroy beauty in the name of bureaucracy. Lady Bird Johnson, you may recall, latched on to highway beautification as her First Lady claim to fame. During her highway beautification movement, roadside signs were deemed

an eyesore. The "Lady Bird Act" meant that many of Rock City's rooftop messages had to be painted over.

As for Mom's Rock City birdhouse, like many a Rock City barn, its best days are behind it. Neglect and decay make for formidable allies, whether you're an aged barn or a souvenir from Pigeon Forge, Tennessee.

I saw Rock City as a boy, and what seems one hundred years later, I can still see a Rock City barn. You can too. An online map of surviving Rock City barns directs you to these survivors (www.seerockcity.com). Georgia has five. North Carolina has six. South Carolina has one, and here it is.

Permit me a fantasy. I'm on a Sunday drive with Mom and Dad in that aqua-and-white '56 Plymouth. Along Highway 28, we look to the left and see a handsome barn with a man on its roof. There's Clark Byers sketching out letters. Dad honks the horn, and Byers turns and waves. He returns to work, using chalk to outline "See 7 States from Rock City. Near Chattanooga Tenn." We just witnessed history in the making, and some sixty years later, I see what's left of Clark Byers's work, a ghostly reminder of times past and one barn that escaped Lady Bird's beautification movement.

Sunday drivers passed this barn on Highway 28 south of Abbeville, South Carolina's only such barn. Georgia has five, North Carolina, six.

HOLIDAY DRIVES

I can't recall the first time I saw an interstate, but I'm sure it frightened me. With a city-like presence, interstates invaded rustic countryside with a vengeance. All that concrete and speed should have scared me. Understand that I grew up in the countryside of two-lane eastern Georgia, gravel-road Georgia, where dirt roads run through cornfields. Come Thanksgiving and Christmas, we never took an interstate anywhere. We drove country roads to visit both sides of the family; these holiday drives were fabulous Sunday-like drives.

In one direction, we drove past red barns leaning with the wind, country stores with wisps of cotton plugging their screen doors, old churches and tenant homes perched at the edge of fields; in another, we passed an old mansion where men robbed the Confederate gold train, a fire tower, vintage log cabins and a swamp where an albino eastern panther once prowled. Those drives fostered memories and stoked my imagination. To this day, their magic holds me in a trance.

Alas, trances are rare. Today, when I merge onto an interstate—that hardened asphalt-cement land of stress—monotony takes control. Gridlock. Plodding along, then rushing headlong at high speed. Long lines of cars and trucks. Exhaust fumes. Hitting the brakes yet again. A maddening hitchhiker named Frustration slides behind the wheel. Those of you who need no airplane tickets come holidays, those of you who drive to see loved ones, if this experience seems all too familiar, I suggest you make a change. Revive the Sunday drive and take a back-road route. Give the little ones something to look at. Give them something they'll remember.

I have rich memories from my boyhood holidays. Come Thanksgiving, dreaming of quail and deer from the back seat of Dad's Plymouth, I watched the fields and forests of eastern Georgia slide by my window. That auburn field of broomstraw surely held quail. That dark line of oaks burdened with acorns? Without doubt a big buck feasted there. The heart-stopping sight of a majestic buck froze me fast. The nerve-jolting flush of a covey exploded in my little boy head.

Come Christmas, I imagined those same fields and forests lacquered in white. I was certain flakes as big as chicken feathers would tumble from the sky on Christmas Eve. Should it snow, I just knew I'd slip outside every ten minutes to measure the accumulating magic, a winter wonderland rare and sublime. I knew an altogether new architecture would redefine all familiar into white lines and soft, glistening curves, for a milky species of kudzu was about to consume the countryside. Red cedars—the only Christmas tree I long knew—stood like dark green sentinels in fields. I imagined their boughs heavy with crusts of snow. I anticipated a white Christmas, a rare time when a veneer of confectioner's sugar would make Christmas all the sweeter, though in truth it never did. Not once. Even so, I hold my snowless holiday drives dear. How about you? Got great holiday drive memories? Do you prefer idling at mile marker 106 or driving a comfy fifty miles per hour along a scenic country road? If time is your goal, a back-road Sunday drive may be a better bet these days. Take an interstate and chances are a traffic jam will force you to exit somewhere anyway.

Along the interstate, you pass through the kingdom of fast-food franchises. Along the back roads, you'll see old gas stations and stores converted to cozy restaurants. Why not map out a memorable holiday drive, one that you and your family will enjoy, one that will give you something to talk about.

Take a Sunday-drive approach to the holidays this season. You stand a far better chance to see steel truss bridges crossing forgotten rivers in a land of beautiful wreckage where old mansions crumble, ghost signs adorn brick walls in sleepy towns and holiday lights promise to overload the circuits. See hawks, wild turkey, deer and coyotes, sleepy cemeteries and shuttered country stores, pecan orchards wreathed in fog and classic old cars mounded up in junkyards. Drive past old gas pumps and country homes where plumes of chimney smoke fill the air with the fragrant incense of oak and hickory. See old train depots and sleepy mill villages.

The benefits of the lesser-traveled roads are not to be ignored. The kids are more apt to ignore their tablets and pads on a country road. All in all, a pleasant trip unfolds, one that adds to the joy of the holidays. Think about a different route for once. If you heed my advice, a Sunday-drive holiday trip might, in fact, become a cherished holiday tradition.

EASTER DAFFODILS

My family made many Sunday drives to see family, something not as common today in this far-flung family era. Back in the 1950s and '60s, Easter Sundays were a given for visiting my grandparents. Despite all those bygone years, a clear memory of one Easter Sunday remains: having my photograph taken. That was a big deal before phones turned cameras. There I am, circa 1957, standing amid green and yellow clumps of daffodils. Dad posed me in their midst for my Easter photo. I stand just so lest I trample the tender stems. Got my new white bucks and Sunday finest on, fresh flattop haircut and a gap-toothed smile, but I best not step on any daffodils, and I best not stain my white suede shoes. Right, Carl?

Dad pushes a button, and the Polaroid makes a whirring noise as the self-developing film slides forth. He peels away a white layer, and there I am. I recall it as if it were yesterday, but it was yesteryear, and the photo? Lost in the dustbin of years gone by.

So I thought. Half a century later, going through my late mother's possessions, I discovered that photo. Beneath a worn leather-bound Bible in a desk hid a yellow-brown photograph: that Polaroid print taken Easter Day, circa 1957. The daffodils were just as I remember. Five clumps. Two in front. Three in back. Those daffodils stand tall in memory, not because I stepped gingerly around them, but because of what happened next.

Out comes Grandmom, and what does she do? She cuts them and goes inside. I stare at the amputated stalks I so carefully avoided, then run into the farmhouse. Grandmom's at the sink putting the daffodils in a Mason jar. Into it she pours blue food coloring. Soon, the flowers draw up the dye, and delicate blue-green tributaries run through spring's golden trumpeters. Each flower soon sports a blue-green corona. Sheer magic. Ever since, seeing daffodils never fails to resurrect Mason jar flowers with aquamarine edges. Of course, daffodils give me the first cue that spring will pry winter's icy fingers from the land, but they never fail to remind me of that Easter when worry gave way to joy.

In the years to come, that daffodil, Easter Sunday drive stayed in my mind as I made other drives connected to flowers. Camellias, however, didn't bloom in my boyhood memory for a simple reason. We had no "cold flowers." As a boy, I believed that to have camellias, you had to live in a mansion with Augusta National–like landscaping. Our grounds consisted of grass, pines and, here and there, honeysuckle, oaks and one magnolia. And then, decades later at Edisto Island, I got an unforgettable introduction to camellias.

As I drove to Edisto Island on a gray January day long ago, a thought occurred to me: "I had a childhood without camellias." (Later in life, Mom would plant many camellias.) My mission was to profile camellia expert Colonel Parker Connor Jr., who lived in a plantation home. (See what I mean?) I found the Colonel on the grounds of 1828 Oak

Beloved clumps of yellow and green greeted many a Sunday driver. Harbinger of spring, daffodils go by narcissus and jonquils.

Island Plantation, a home overlooking the marsh. The morning was cool as we walked the grounds. Colonel Connor pointed to a delicate blossom. "That's a Miss Charleston." As the Colonel pointed out other camellias—"Dawn's Early Light, Boutonniere, Walterboro and Wildwood"—I decided I would grow camellias, too, and when I had my yards landscaped, I put in a dozen camellias.

My interest in camellias blossomed. That, in part, led me to make another flower-connected drive: a trip to the camellia tea in Edgefield. At a historic home, Magnolia Dale, we sipped tea from the Charleston Tea Plantation, and beautiful blooms, properly annotated, brought the classic South alive. Polished silver tea sets gleamed as window light struck them. Faces in oil on canvas gazed at participants. It was an occasion, a flowery, beautiful occasion.

The beautiful camellias could never have rivals, you'd think, but you'd be wrong. I present dogwoods and their snow-white blossoms. When Mom talked about dogwoods, you could not miss the excitement in her voice. She loved them, and we didn't have to drive to see one. We long had a stately dogwood near the old propane tank that banished many a winter's frigid air. I loved that tree's snow-white emblematic blossoms that a botanist will tell you are bracts, not blossoms. Mom and her dogwood are no more, but in the spring when I make long drives down gravel roads through deep forests, I see snowstorm-like cottony dogwoods popping out in dark woods. They spirit me back to my long-gone Georgia childhood.

Lord, Lord, change never stops. That sink where Grandmom poured blue food coloring into a Mason jar? Well, it lies in ashes. Her house burned a few years back. Nothing from childhood remains except memories of Easter Sunday drives, and even that yellow-brown Polaroid print taken by my late father is no more. Misplaced. "All gone," as kids will say.

Well, we carry on, don't we. Come spring, daffodils will rise through the ashes of Grandmom's old home. Those daffodils will convince me winter is giving way to spring, and something more. Flowers outlast us. When we are in the ground or our ashes scattered or imprisoned in some urn or box, daffodils, camellias and dogwoods will keep bringing beauty to the land. Someday, a boy not yet born will stand in his own clumps of daffodils while his dad takes a photo with some digital device. As for me, each Easter that I can, I'll go back to those same daffodils in new white bucks. I'll set up my Canon and take one of those "then and now" photographs. All the while, I'll be careful not to trample the great-great-grandblooms of those original daffodils, for the old ways, well, they sure die hard, don't they.

Christmas Tree Adventures

For many years, my father ran his own business, a chainsaw shop where he repaired small gasoline engines and welded all manner of metal objects. My first regular job was working in Dad's saw shop on Saturdays. The shop was a tin building with no insulation. It broiled in summers. Winters turned its concrete floor into a slab of ice. Neither heat nor cold, though, stopped pulpwooders from bringing their dead and dying chainsaws to Dad's shop, where he and his partner, Bobby Cooper, repaired them. Before they could work miracles with vices, screwdrivers and wrenches, it fell on me to remove the gummy black pine resin from covers protecting the saw's inner workings. I swirled a paintbrush in a can holding about three inches of gas and then, on bended knees on concrete, sloshed gas over the saws and scraped away the stubborn black gunk—resin, sawdust and oil—with a screwdriver. I'd take the covers off, which meant skinned knuckles and fingernails caked with grease. It never failed that one bolt refused to budge, frustrating Dad. He would have to stop the important work to help me.

I did not like this work. I smelled like gasoline. All Saturday I cleaned saws and occasionally lawnmowers. On summer Saturdays, I imagined other boys my age were playing baseball, and if they weren't playing baseball, they were at the lake swimming. If it was winter, I knew they were inside and warm reading a good book. Or if, like me, they had to work, they worked in grocery stores bagging canned goods, bread and milk, and their hands were free of grease, grime and gasoline, plus they were getting tips. Wherever they were, their lot was better than mine. At the end of a long Saturday, I wondered just where I had gone wrong.

Dad worked six days a week—Monday through Saturday—but as Christmas approached, I knew that one Sunday soon, we'd head out to my granddad's farm to cut a Christmas tree. That made late November Saturdays easier to tolerate, and it made something else—memories. Many years later, those memories came to me in a cold attic. My sisters and I were sorting through our late parents' things. In that dim, dusty attic, Christmases past surrounded me. Like Dickens's old *Christmas Carol*, ghosts of sorts surrounded me: ornaments, wreathes and red velvet boughs hung from the rafters with care…and one artificial tree.

I don't know why Mom and Dad quit putting up a real tree. I suppose artificial trees became fashionable. One thing's for sure, the era of plastic trees with built-in lights saved many a tree on Granddad's farm. The various artificial trees were perfectly shaped and beautiful, but I missed an eastern red cedar cut from the farm. One whiff of its needles, and I knew Christmas was at hand.

We'd head out beneath a cold sky seeking the perfect eastern red cedar. When a boy, there was no better day than a cold Sunday on the farm beneath a gray quilted sky hinting of snow. (When I was a kid, all winter skies hinted of snow. But it never snowed on Christmas. Never.) Sometimes we jumped a covey of quail or a rabbit, and now and then a hawk would fly over. We were in the midst of nature, no traffic or fluorescent lights. No crowds. None whatsoever. Back then, we would move from one field to another, stopping to open the old gap gates made of cedar poles and three strands of barbed wire. No big metal gates existed then.

Farm cedars almost always had a "hole" due to how they grew. Like a stunning woman with a facial scar, it made them more real than perfect, yet fake, trees. Mom and Dad would turn the hole to the wall and string bubble cane lights and icicles onto the fresh green boughs, and I'd watch as the lights bubbled, reflecting off the icicles. No lights will ever top those. Now Christmas lights are LEDs. Artificial trees don't smell like Christmas, and you get them at Walmart or on a street corner beneath a string of naked light bulbs. What fun.

When Christmas was over, we hauled the tree into the woods, where nature took its course. Now people in the cities hold "grinding of the greens" or chop them into short lengths and the garbage guys haul it off—a sad demise.

One Thanksgiving, I spent four days at my daughter Beth's place in Apex, North Carolina. The day after Thanksgiving, we headed out to find a Christmas tree. That meant to a "farm" overrun with people. So many people, in fact, that traffic needed a policeman to manage things. But there was no policeman. No problem; my son-in-law, Chris, found a way to get us into the farm. We parked, got out and found ourselves in the midst of a crowd.

The trees, shipped in from North Carolina mountains, leaned here and there. Trees everywhere. We walked through a relocated forest. Families appraised them, and when the right tree was found, a fellow on a Polaris ATV hauled it to a shed, where loose needles were shaken free and the trunk's base was cut and squared, then wrapped in netting for the trip home. Cheap they were not. Granddad's cedars? Free. A true Christmas gift.

It beat a fake tree by a mile. Beth and her family got the tree home and put it up, and without doubt it was beautiful. What bothers me though is the fact that her children have no memories of exploring a real farm, looking for the right tree. I, however, do. The entire time we were getting the tree, my mind was back in Lincoln County, Georgia, more precisely at Granddad Poland's farm. Come Christmas in the 1950s, we'd head down Double Branches Road to the farm. There, we got in a battered car and headed through the pastures to the edges of fields where red cedars stood like sentries, like soldiers moved to the front of Shakespeare's Birnam Wood. We'd look and look and eventually find the right tree. Dad would cut it, and those needles and gold drops of resin filled the chill air with the original fragrance of Christmas.

One night, a woman asked me what I wanted for Christmas. I thought a bit. "Nothing. I have all I need or want." Then I thought and an answer came to me: "A return to Christmas trees cut from woods."

Those few of you with real trees and vintage lights like my parents once used, you old-timers you? Thank you. Without doubt you will have a Merry Christmas, a traditional Christmas, one filled with the fragrance of a forest. Not polyvinyl chloride.

SAWDUST PILES

In the Sunday drive era, we often saw sawdust piles. I never see sawdust piles anymore—yet another bit of the past that's slipped away. Sawdust piles hold magic and nostalgia for me. Each morning, I woke to the sound of Mr. Henry Partridge's sawmill planing lumber. It sounded like a big cicada, a rising and falling whine I've not heard since.

Saturdays, I'd walk through the woods to the old sawmill. There it stood, a glistening, pine-scented pile, shaped by the "angle of repose." I long wanted to climb that beautiful pile of sawdust with its fancy angle of repose but was scared to—with reason, as you've read, although it didn't discourage others.

As I remembered Mr. Henry's sawmill, I wanted to see one, maybe even climb it. At the very least, I decided, I'd find one to photograph. No luck. Today, trains and trucks haul off sawdust. Every so often, I drive up behind a big truck carting sawdust down the road. The sawdust piles we used to see end up shipped to places that use sawdust to make things like particleboard, an engineered wood product.

Where, I wondered, can I find a sawdust pile? I put out a request: "Does anyone know where an old sawdust pile is?" Only one person could locate one, but it was a piece away, as the old folks used to say. Plenty of memories surfaced, however.

High school friend Ronnie Myers wrote to me: "Daddy knew where several were in the vicinity of his house and he would go get old sawdust for mulching his grape vineyard 30 or 40 years ago, and even then they had deteriorated to a point that they were almost flat. The ones I knew of would surely be unrecognizable by now."

McCormick's Linda McComb Floyd wrote to me too: "We had one on our farm Dad used and gave away for mulch. Lost many a flip-flop sliding down the sawdust pile."

Ronnie passed along some good advice: "Talk to Gary Ward. In the 50s and 60s his daddy, Pelham, had 'portable' sawmills where you took the sawmill onto someone's property and cut their timber onsite. On big tracts of timber they would be sawing lumber for several weeks or months at a time and that's where you would have large piles of sawdust. Foxes and other woodland critters loved old sawdust piles because they could dig burrows and tunnels in them for dens. Potatoes grew well in them also."

My friend Debby Johnston Summey of Georgetown wrote to me: "In the rural area where my family lived, there were several giant sawdust piles. As children, we were warned not to climb the piles as they could collapse and suffocate us."

High school colleague and friend Skip Hardin added an ominous note to the warning not to play on a sawdust pile: "There use to be one behind Lauren Mims' house that we spent many hours playing on. As I remember, the real terror story was that deep in the bowels of the sawdust pile it could catch fire from spontaneous combustion and a hapless lad could be playing on it when it would collapse and he'd be sucked into an inferno. That prospect got my attention but not so much that it prevented us from playing on it."

Plummeting into an inferno—that sounds a bit like dropping into Hades, does it not?

I was happy to see Gary Ward join our discussion because he possesses more than a bit of knowledge about all matters sawmill and sawdust. Said Gary, "Portable sawmills were all over this area in the late 40s, not so many in the 50s as most of the timber was cut out of this area. Clark [sic] Hill Lake took up a huge portion of the timber-producing area. There was a resurgence of mills in the early 60s as more timber matured. By the early 70s, almost all of these mills were gone. The sawdust piles from this era have pretty much deteriorated until there is almost nothing left. Skip is right that they could get hot enough to burn due to the composting. But if they did catch fire, they mostly would just simmer along because the fire would not get enough oxygen to burn. It was a lot of fun playing on sawdust piles!"

Gary said, "The old 'pecker wood' mills were not very efficient. Typically, the lumber was cut and stacked for air-drying right in the woods at the mill site. When dry, it would be hauled to planer mills such as Cullers Lumber Company, Dorn Lumber Company in McCormick, or Cox Lumber

Company in Troy, South Carolina. They could not operate in one place for more than a few weeks before the sawdust and other waste started getting in the way. Then they would have to move the mill, even if only a short distance away. But the entire operation could be moved in one day. It became more efficient to haul the logs to large stationary mills such as Pollard Lumber Company or the mill my father and I ran in McCormick. And that's more than you wanted to know about saw milling!"

Big piles of sawdust—yet another thing today's kids miss out on. I remember walking into the edge of Mr. Henry's sawdust pile just a bit. Sort of like the ocean, I didn't want to go in too deep for fear of the unknown. As a kid, I wanted to climb its very top, but I didn't. Like Debbie, I had been warned you could fall into its collapsing midst and suffocate. No guts, no glory, as they say. I should have climbed it.

Sawdust piles. At least I have memories. I can still hear that old mill working, though. A rising and falling sound like a giant cicada.

SAWMILLING

I was standing by the tracks in front of the old Hotel Keturah in McCormick, South Carolina. A train blast sounded. Coming up from the south was a CSX train with many a car filled with fresh sawdust, so fresh the glistening chips looked wet, so fresh they filled the air with the scent of pine resin. "There go more of my boyhood sawdust piles," I thought, and sure enough, each car sported a pile of sawdust destined to become particleboard.

Yes, many Sunday drives took us past a sawdust pile, and each time they did I wanted to get out of the car and climb that pile of chips. A sawdust pile held more appeal than a playground back then when portable sawmills turned trees into man's products. That's not the case today. I'm reminded of this change now and then when I sit at my three-hundred-year-old longleaf heartpine table. The wood is beautiful, and you can see the old saw marks.

Well, thanks to Katherine Bray of Milledgeville, Georgia, I appreciate my table even more. Katherine read one of my columns and sent me memories of her dad's sawmilling years. Now I know how hard it was to get the wood for my table. Her story takes place in Hancock County, Georgia, from the 1920s into the early 1940s, but it could be Lincoln County, Georgia; McCormick, South Carolina; or Robeson, North Carolina, just as easily. The recollection of her father's work proves quite revealing. The next time you go to Home Depot, Lowes or a local hardware store for decking boards or two-by-fours, remember Katherine's dad and all he and his co-workers had to endure. Here are excerpts from Katherine's "Sawmilling—A Hard Life."

"The cutting of timber was a big industry in Hancock County during the 1920s, 1930s, and early 1940s. That is why my father came here from Taliaferro County when he was only 17 to live with his sister and brother-in-law and to have a job."

Her dad learned a lot about sawmilling, and with a bank loan and help from a planing mill owner, he was able to get his own sawmill. At the peak of the industry, there were as many as forty portable sawmills in the county. "In the early years of his sawmilling he was not able to come home every night due to the distance and long working hours. He and his hands stayed in whatever building they could find nearby and this was called 'shacking.' Often it was an abandoned farm building of some type. Most of the hands slept on pallets or straw, but Daddy had a cot, which folded under at each end. On this he had a feather mattress he slept on and quilts for cover."

The men had a kitchen they pulled from one site to another, a wooden shack on wheels. It had a wood stove, a wooden table and a chair. "Robert, the only cook I remember, had gotten too old to work at the mill. Breakfast consisted of fried fat back, sawmill gravy, biscuits, and branch water. The eating utensils consisted of tin forks and spoons, enamel cups and plates."

She wrote of how the men supplemented meals with game. "Rabbit boxes were set out or someone would kill squirrels. In the summer watermelons would be brought from home, placed in a creek to cool and cut after supper. After supper everyone was so tired they immediately went to sleep and I never heard Daddy say a word about not being able to go to sleep." The men's day began at daybreak and ended at sundown.

Nothing concerning sawmilling was easy. "On Monday morning, Daddy would arise at 4 o'clock and start a fire in the wood stove. Mother would cook him breakfast and fix him a lunch in his tin lunch box. Everyone had to carry a lunch on Monday because they would not arrive at the sawmill site in time for Robert to cook."

In winter, the men had to drain water from the Model T radiator. A kettle of warm water would be poured into the radiator, and her dad would hand crank the "strip down," a truck without a top that had planks on the floor and sides. "This was cold riding on these wintry mornings. He would leave about daybreak to travel 12 or 15 miles picking up hands along the way. Sometimes there would be so many men standing by the road wanting a job that some had to be refused. Since times were so hard people were willing to work just for something to eat and a place to sleep."

And then there were the mules, bless 'em. When a sawmill moved to another location, the men built a lot near a branch so the mules would have plenty of water. They built feed troughs. Planks and a strand of barbed wire made for a lot. Wrote Katherine, "Feeding my Daddy's sawmill mules was the first paying job some boys had." Sawmill mules were different from farm mules. "Sawmill mules had larger flanks for pulling much heavier loads than the farm mules. A 'snaking' mule pulled the logs to a clearing in the woods where the logs were stacked."

As for time off, there wasn't much. "Only two holidays were observed during these hard-time years," she wrote. On the Fourth of July, there would be a fish fry on a nearby creek. The other holiday, of course, was Christmas. "Daddy would buy loose candy, a sack of oranges and apples, and dried raisins with stems. He always knew how many children were in each family and they were given a sack of 'goodies' and a little extra piece of money."

"Today," writes Katherine, "we see trucks hauling 'spindly' logs and I think about all the virgin timber that was cut in years past. Some logs were as large as four feet at the base. This was a hard livelihood for Daddy but he enjoyed looking at pine trees all his life. During his sawmilling years only certain size trees were harvested so the smaller ones could grow. You would have another stand of timber in a few years."

So ends Katherine's recollection, a narrative that applies to many counties in Georgia, South Carolina and North Carolina. Sawmilling has changed, as we've seen. Pulpwood mills remain in one place now, and huge trucks bring the logs to the mills. The days of hard-earned lumber, when felling a tree took muscle, sweat and courage, are gone. One fellow can clear a large forest from a comfortable seat up high in a modern hydraulic machine. Just the other day I drove by a clearcut. You could see the tracks of bulldozers and the big power density harvesters. It looked like a battlefield. Nary a mule witnessed the cutting of those woods.

HOMEMADE TOYS

I t was like cutting through steel. I had to get out my electric Black & Decker scissors to cut through the hard, clear plastic that encased remote-controlled helicopters for my grandsons. As I cut the helicopters free, I thought, "Man, we had nothing like these when I was a boy." And then I went back to the days when toys encased in hard, clear plastic didn't exist. I went back to the days when we made our own toys.

As a kid, nothing thrilled me more than a thick stand of bamboo. Emerald green and tropical, the tall, strong culms transported me to jungles where headhunters shot poison darts from blowguns. But there was another reason to be excited—a better reason. Those jade stalks, with a little work, could be turned into peashooters and flutes. The key to converting this amazing plant to toys was simple: cut the straightest stalk you could find and saw it off inside the joints, which were solid. A beautiful, natural tube resulted.

I made slingshots for my grandsons, which fascinated them. As a kid, I didn't go anywhere without my slingshot. It rested in my hip pocket, and in one fluid motion, I could whip it out and send a piece of gravel flying at a rusty old can.

A close cousin to the slingshot was a rubber band pistol. Easy to make. Draw a pistol-like design onto a pine board, cut it out with a handsaw, sand it a bit, nail a wooden clothespin on top for a trigger and cut a notch in the end of the barrel. Cut some stout rubber bands from an inner tube, and you had added yet another weapon to your arsenal. Getting smacked by a rubber

Green tropical stands of bamboo provided kids peashooters, flutes and fishing poles.

band didn't hurt. Today, making a toy gun is politically just cause to expel a kid and pack him off to a counselor to work out his so-called anger issues.

Another great homemade toy was a "tractor" made from a wooden spool of thread, a matchstick, a rubber band and an ice cream stick. By the way, you'll be hard-pressed to find a wooden spool of thread today; they're all plastic. Making a tractor from a wooden spool was simple. Cut notches into the spool's outer flanges, insert a rubber band and secure it on one end with the matchstick and the ice cream stick on the other. Wind up the ice cream stick, then set it down and watch it roll off. It could even go uphill.

Nothing fascinated me like magnets as a kid. To this day, I maintain that a magnet is about the most fascinating object on the planet. I used to tie magnets to a string and loop the string over a nail in a door, and just like that I had a boy's version of a tall crane, able to lift loads of tacks, whatever small metal objects I could find. Boys in the 1950s truly loved magnets. The band members in Pink Floyd grew up about the same time I did, and they paid homage to magnets' power to inspire in a song called "High Hopes": "In a world of magnets and miracles, our thoughts strayed constantly and without boundary…" How true. Nothing worked my imagination like a strong magnet.

Another simple toy we made was a dart fashioned from a matchstick, a straight pin and paper. We'd cut slits into the matchstick and insert paper fins, cut off the match head and insert the pin. These little darts were deadly, laser beams of accuracy.

We made parachutes from bandanas and rocks. Throw them into the air and watch them drift to earth.

Making your own toys was a fine tradition. My dad told me many times how he and his friends used a simple iron hoop from a barrel as a toy. They'd get it rolling and keep it rolling with a stick that guided it.

Looking back, one of the darker days in my life, a day that marked a big change, came from a cereal box. Perhaps you remember the deep-sea divers billed as diving frogmen. You'd put baking soda into a compartment under their feet, drop them into water and watch them bob up and down. Why a dark day? Because it was a sign of things to come: the advent of plastic and mass-produced toys. The 1950s gave us plastic hula-hoops, Silly Putty, Mr. Potato Head and, by the end of the decade, plastic Barbie dolls.

Before plastic and batteries came along, before Walmart and Toys R Us existed, we made do. Folks made dolls for little girls from cornhusks. We made simple propellers from small blocks of pine. Carve out the blade and drill a hole in the middle where a loose-fitting nail attached it to a wooden handle. Hold it out the car window and listen to it go.

We kids of the 1950s were "green" before green was cool. Just about all of our toys were biodegradable and Earth friendly, and they didn't depend on batteries. Bamboo, cornhusks and wood break down. You can't say that for plastic toys. Broken and abandoned by kids, a plastic toy buried in a landfill can take hundreds of years to break down. And just imagine how many batteries end up in landfills each year.

We made our own toys back in the day, and in a way, our little inventions made us. Entertaining yourself with a toy fashioned from scraps of lumber or a fine piece of bamboo made you feel good about yourself. It boosted your self-esteem. "Hey, look. I made this."

We did little harm with our delightful do-it-yourself toys, I might add, and today's economists would have looked on our homemade toys with an approving eye. We weren't consumers; we were manufacturers. In the true spirit of American ingenuity and capitalism, we filled a void with a much-needed product.

Our digital-dependent kids? They're one of the country's most coveted consumer markets. And that means that bamboo has nothing to fear.

COKE BOTTLE IMPROVISATIONS

The year was 1958. On a cutting board next to a white enamel sink, Mom pounded fresh red cube steak with a green Coca-Cola bottle. She was tenderizing it. On other days, she used that bottle capped with a perforated top to sprinkle water across white cotton shirts. As she ironed, the crisp fragrance of steaming cotton filled the kitchen. Back then, Mom and many others used old Coke bottles in inventive ways. Those thick, green-glass bottles lived on once their sweet carbonated drinks vanished. You can bet your bottom dollar that Coke bottle wasn't going to end up in a stream, lake, the sea or a landfill.

Back then, we drank from thick, strong, useful glass bottles. I hammered a nail into a board with a Coke bottle once. You could even buy an aluminum sprinkler with a cork that fit snugly in the bottle. Those days are gone with the winds of change. Folks back then found ways to get by. Plastic had yet to invade their lives, nor had steam irons. Innovation was the order of the day. Aren't you weary of plastic? I am. I'm tired of plastic grocery bags, plastic water bottles, plastic soft drink bottles, cheap plastic toys and plastic litter everywhere I look. I would love to see glass resurgent.

Mom's old Coke bottle? It carried a deposit. Seems it ran from two cents a bottle to a nickel. We boys would scour the roadsides for bottles. Entrepreneurs we were. You didn't see soft drink bottles along the roads when I was a boy. That would have been like seeing money out by the highways. Now you see thin, flimsy plastic water bottles and other plastic debris everywhere you look. I was about to photograph a whitewater river a

few years back. Looking through the viewfinder, there it was: a bright orange water cooler jug lodged against a rock. I go into swamps, and even there I can't escape it. In blackwater swamps, plastic water bottles bob among cypress knees. The only wild places where I escape plastic bags and bottles are Carolina bays.

How many times do you see a red plastic gas can along the road where it flew out of a pickup? If they were made of heavy-gauge metal like they once were, that wouldn't happen. Bring back metal, too. I see plastic grocery bags snagged in trees all the time. Enough is enough.

You probably recycle. I recycle plastic—aluminum, too, anything I can— but as my friend Lee Brockington of Hobcaw Barony observed, "Recycling is no longer enough."

We need to get rid of the stuff, but until that happens, just quit buying the junk. I keep a permanent water bottle handy. I fill it up whenever I go afield or do yard work.

I don't care what the plastic association folks and lobbyists say; our own two eyes tell us plastic is a menace. Sea turtles swathed in plastic netting, pelicans ensnared in plastic bags—all that has created the need to police beaches and waterways. All roads led to Rome and all waterways lead to the sea, and that's where plastic ends up.

We're entombed in plastic. I am fine with plastic in phones, computers and car interiors. But when you give people plastic forks, spoons and drink straws, too many people toss them away. Man has yet to develop a pesticide that kills litterbugs.

We got rid of pop-tops on aluminum beverage cans. Now we need to severely reduce our use of plastic. Use a water bottle that is uniquely yours. Buy the permanent grocery bags and use 'em. (I miss the heavy-duty paper bags; found a lot of uses for them.)

Stand a classic Coca-Cola bottle beside a flimsy plastic water bottle. The difference you see carries a name: art. Art that you, nature and I appreciate.

One more thing. When we took Sunday drives in the 1950s, we never saw plastic trash along the roadways.

Between 1886 and 1959, a 6.5-ounce glass or bottle of Coca-Cola was just a nickel for a cold treat.

OLD-FASHIONED PETUNIAS

Vintage petunias. I had forgotten those flowers Grandma loved. Surely I saw them in my youth. As I sort through my mental album, I think I recall them. Pale colors, pastel petals of white and pink, possibly lavender, and a delicate softness. Seems Grandmother Walker grew them on her porch, a wide, columned porch destined to burn. There, on that doomed veranda, they grew in pots, over-spilling, upside down, their blooms a bit like inverted antebellum skirts. In the flowers' throats, dark veins converged, a floral case of perspective.

How long ago I forgot about those old-timey petunias. A lot of time passed, and then suddenly I couldn't escape them. A woman down Florida way spotted them in my photograph of a country store along old U.S. 1. "Did you notice the old-timey petunias by the store's steps?"

I brought up the photo, and there they were, a cluster of ten or so, frozen by the shutter, flowers dancing in an old Disney cartoon classic. For some reason, all faced away from the sun, gazing at their own shadows. And then I discovered vintage petunias a week ago at an old homeplace. Discovered them in person in a large field adjacent to the ruins of an old tenant home.

I wrote about Miss Johnnie who loved trains, and the trainman who visited this woman who waved at the trains said this: "I walked through Miss Johnnie's fragrant purple old-timey petunias; the perennial kind our southern grandmothers grew in their yards."

That would be correct.

You don't see them as much these days, but when you least expect it, vintage petunias will surprise you at an old store or homesite.

Old-fashioned petunias, what I refer to as Grandma's petunias, are still out there, straight from childhood. This hardy, aromatic heirloom flower hints of old homeplaces, and indeed, that's where I stumbled upon them. Think of them as vintage flowers. I recall my late mom talking about old-fashioned petunias and a flower that has a beautiful name, delphinium, oh, and plumbago too. Finally, I saw old petunias in person and this time recognized them for what they are: vintage flowers.

That hot afternoon in the front yard of what was once a tenant home, I leaned over and breathed in their scent. I can best describe it as a green spicy peppery fragrance, similar to something you might cook with. It didn't overpower me, and I liked that. I had to work to gather its incense. Modern hybrids, alas, have no fragrance.

So, what happens to these old flowers when the people who planted them are no more? They keep on keeping on. Perched atop long stalks, they reseed themselves. And reseed themselves. Things change. Homes burn. Homes suffering abandonment decay. People die, but the flowers keep on keeping on. Old homeplaces and forgotten cemeteries still harbor these flowers. Deprived of someone to water them, fertilize them and keep harmful insects away, they get by on their own.

I say it's time we planted more petunias, the kind Grandma loved. Old-fashioned petunias possess a heritage, and they're survivors. They'll be here when you and I will not.

HOME REMEDIES

On our Sunday drives into the countryside, we never saw hospitals, urgent care clinics or docs-in-a-box. Well, people got sick and injured back then too. What did they do? They used home remedies. Case in point: a stern grandmother leans over a little boy who's frowning. Grandma, clad in a white gown with her hair all bunched up, aims a spoonful of castor oil at the boy's mouth, clamped tight, of course. Medicine was never supposed to taste good, but this stuff is outright horrible.

In some homes, and this grandma's no exception, the first sniffle of a cold brought on a dose of castor oil. I don't know if castor oil helped, but with healthcare such a mess and modern medicine costing so much, it wouldn't surprise me to see a return to "Grandma's Remedies." Perhaps remedies based on experience and knowledge passed from generation to generation offer some alternatives to modern medicine and its pricey insurance-entangling ways. There's some time-tested truth behind old remedies, and that's what made some of them work. Indians would chew willow bark to alleviate pain. Today, we know a true miracle drug was in that bark: acetylsalicylic acid (salicin). Aspirin.

Of course, many a charlatan has cashed in on fake medicines that claim to heal anything from a hangnail to a headache to vertigo to vomiting. There's a great scene in that classic film *The Outlaw Josey Wales*. A traveling medicine man in a white suit hawks a bottle of elixir that will cure anything. Josey Wales rides up, and the huckster tells Wales his tonic "can do most anything."

Folks collect old medicine bottles today, but in yesteryear, they dispensed home remedies.

Wales scowls and spits a stream of dark tobacco on the man's suit. "How is it with stains?" Wales rides off. He had reason to spit. The tonics of yesteryear promised to cure everything from baldness to rashes and colds, and most were chock-full of alcohol, so a buzz might have made people feel something medicinal was going on. Cures? Never.

Closely related to snake oil salesmen's wares were patent medicines. Two made it into literature. In *Deliverance*, James Dickey resurrected two cures from the past, one of which it so happened his family had owned at one time: Black Draught. As the men drive toward the hill country, there's this passage: "There was a motel, then a weed field, and then on both sides Clabber Girl came out of hiding, leaping onto the sides of barns, 666 and Black Draught began to swirl, and Jesus began to save."

Devilish-sounding 666 claimed to cure malaria (later colds), and Black Draught was a common commercial liquid syrup laxative, a purgative made from a blend of senna and magnesia. Like castor oil, Black Draught was a commonly used folk remedy for many ailments. (A young Dolly Parton sang a jingle for the product: "Smile from the inside out, smile from the inside out, Black Draught makes you smile from the inside out.")

Folks in older times loved their patent medicines. Granddad Poland wouldn't be caught without his Doans Pills. They came in a small green metal canister and relieved the pain of an aching back—at least that was the claim. He also kept a jar of Vicks VapoRub beneath his pillow so he could breathe better. Like Brylcreme, just a dab would do. Vicks VapoRub, by the way, supposedly treats nail fungus.

Back in my youth, an old fellow wearing a straw hat with a green sunshade often came to Dad's saw shop. He got rid of a wart on my left thumb by rubbing a broomstraw over it while muttering words that made no sense. He broke the straw in half and told me to go into the woods and throw that half over my left shoulder and never look at it again. I did, and a month or so later, the wart was gone.

Here are some old remedies that kept our predecessors from going to the doctor or at least provided fairly cheap relief. Cigarette tobacco, moistened and applied as a poultice, took the sting out of bee stings. Having trouble being "regular"? Try prune juice. (I have a friend who swears that Coca-Cola does the trick.)

Another friend recalls that her dad would make a hot toddy of liquor, lemon juice and sugar to banish colds. "It knocked us out and we slept a lot," she said. Akin to this remedy is one that cures a sore throat. Mix a fourth of a cup of honey with a fourth of a cup of whiskey.

When I was a boy, I went through a spell of boils. Dr. Pennington would lance them, and that was no fun. A home remedy for boils involves applying tomato paste to a boil. Supposedly the acid in tomatoes brings the boil to a head while alleviating the pain.

Some "cures" sound farfetched. A unique suggestion for curing a headache is placing an ice-cold piece of cooking foil on your forehead. One doctor who studied headaches said the foil cools the blood and the headache disappears in about two minutes.

Here are some other "home" remedies friends remember.

Peppermint and moonshine: Get the old kind of peppermint you had to break with a hammer and let it dissolve in a glass of moonshine. Imbibe. It cures toothaches, coughs and any other aches or pains.

Fire ant bites: Make a poultice out of Adolph's meat tenderizer and water. Rub it on the bites and let it "sit" for fifteen to thirty minutes. It'll keep the bites from forming pustules and turning into sores.

Nose bleeds: Soak a brown paper bag in water and tear some off. Fold it and put it under your upper lip. It works.

Many of us remember how a string tied to a tooth and doorknob circumvented an expensive trip to the dentist. Other such remedies are out there. Myriad teas, tinctures, lotions and ointments sufficed in the old days, and as the old saying goes, "If it was good enough for Grandpa, it's good enough for me."

EATING DIRT

The heyday of Sunday drives was a simpler time when people sought ways to care for their health—odd ways sometimes. I learned of one such way from my days working at Goolsby's country store. That store was a portal to a sometimes-strange world, and one of the stranger things I heard came out of the mouth of Bill Goolsby, a true character. Bill ran the register. He was a good-humored prankster who soldered a quarter to a nail and drove it into the floor near the snack rack. How many laughs I got from the kids and adults who tried to scrape that quarter off the floor. Bill's pranks and wild tales kept me in stitches, so it was hard to believe him when I said, "A lot of folks sure do buy Niagara Starch."

"They eat it," said Bill.

"Eat it?"

"Yep, they eat it."

That's the truth. People white and black ate Niagara Starch back in the Sunday drive era. Starch was a substitute for white dirt, which they preferred but was hard to get. Many times I looked for Niagara Starch in country stores. There it was, waiting for freshly laundered clothes and more than a few appetites. Now don't be so quick to say you would never eat dirt. You already have. Read on.

Folks in the South, particularly Georgia, eat dirt referred to as white clay. Now we're not talking about young girls baking mud pies in Easy Bake ovens. No, eating dirt is a custom slaves brought here from Africa. Other names for white dirt include clay dirt, white clay, kaolin, porcelain clay, china clay, chalk or the scientific aluminum silicate hydroxide. Kaolin is a white clay found mainly in Georgia and Alabama. Sandersville, Georgia, is the Kaolin Capital of the World. And yes, you may well have consumed some of Sandersville's finest white dirt. If you ever taken Kaopectate to stave off a bad stomach, you've eaten dirt. Up until 1980, kaolin was the primary ingredient in Kaopectate. Easy to see how it got its name. Kaolin isn't in Kaopectate anymore, but generic brands still contain it. Read the labels. You'll see.

Kaolin is also in some brands of toothpaste and in Rolaids, Di-gel, Mylanta and Maalox. Of course, using these products doesn't come anywhere close to eating bona fide dirt, which people gladly do. In fact, some people crave white dirt, saying it tastes the way the earth smells when a cloud comes up.

So, how about you non-Kaopectate users? Have you eaten dirt? I'll save you the suspense. The answer is "yes." Kaolin is used in commercial ice cream. That might not be a bad thing. Marc Lallanilla wrote a feature for ABC News, "Eating Dirt: It Might Be Good for You." Here's an excerpt from his feature.

"It melts in your mouth like chocolate," says Ruth Anne T. Joiner, describing the delicious taste of clay around her home in Montezuma. "The good stuff is real smooth. It's just like a piece of candy."

In 1984, the *New York Times* ran a story on the southern practice of eating dirt. "It's after a rainfall, when the earth smells so rich and damp and flavorful, that Fannie Glass says she most misses having some dirt to eat. 'It just always tasted so good to me. When it's good and dug from the right place, dirt has a fine sour taste.'"

There was a time rural women would season dirt with salt and vinegar and eat a handful. And guess what? If they couldn't find dirt, some women use packaged raw cornstarch. Thus did options like Niagara Starch, which has a similar paste-like texture to fine clays, come into play.

It might be good for you. Now if you think there's a fancy term for swallowing soil as therapy, you're right. It's referred to as "geophagy" or "geophagia." From the ancient Greeks to Native Americans, cultures have long practiced geophagy. Women predominantly eat dirt, especially pregnant women. Though medical professionals rarely advocate eating dirt, some nutritionists believe eating clay absorbs toxins due to its binding effect.

Do you wish you had some delicious dirt? Search online for the number-one brand of white dirt, "Grandmas." How about this tagline: "Enjoy a Little Sunshine in Every Bag." There's this bit of salesmanship from the good folks down in White Plains, Georgia: "Tasting Is Believing."

Maybe so. Maybe, too, you should know that according to *Dixie's Forgotten People: The South's Poor Whites*, by J. Wayne Flynt, eating dirt was common among poor whites in the Southeast. Down here, geophagy might have be linked to hookworm disease, of which the desire to eat soil is a symptom.

All this business of craving non-food items falls under a medical term known as pica, pronounced "peeka." Pica derives from the word *magpie*, "a bird thought to eat most anything." As well, magpie comes from the Greek *kissa magpie*, which translates to "false appetite." (Sounds like Latin for "kiss a crow.") In the early 1300s, pica was used to address the phenomenon of women—pregnant women typically—who craved non-food substances.

Before you rush down to Washington County, Georgia, with a shovel, be advised that eating dirt carries a stigma. Eat dirt and some suspect you're, well, dirt poor. That shame discourages many from eating dirt, but a diet of clay might do more for us than we imagine. I've long believed there's a lot of hard-earned wisdom backing customs like acupuncture and clay eating. Who among us, for instance, could sally forth and know which plants in the wild are edible? Not many. Well, animals do that every day without reliance on books, classes or doctors, and animals eat clay. Instinctively drawn to clay, many plant-eating animals eat it after ingesting herbs loaded with toxic tannins.

Research clay eating and you will come across a good many books devoted to clay's healing effects. Downing some dirt has even made its way into literature. In *The Grapes of Wrath*, one of John Steinbeck's main characters gets caught red-handed eating dirt. Dirt is also part of the diet for a character in Pearl Buck's novel *The Good Earth*, an apropos title.

Those country folk long ago at Mr. Clifford's store? History stands by their side. And here in these modern times, women love to apply clay cosmetic masks to their face.

Ready to give white dirt a whirl? Just don't blame me if you get sick. Some physicians warn that you could end up with a ruptured colon. Eat dirt and you might end up in it six feet down. If it does taste like the fragrance of the first few drops from a thunderstorm, I just might order a bag of white dirt and give it a try. On second thought, maybe I'll try some starch first. Whether you entertain that notion or not, the next time you drive through the country, maybe you'll pass through a time warp and find a true country store open. Stop in and ask if they sell Niagara Starch for people to eat. The answer just might surprise you.

SCREEN-WIRE SWATTERS

In Sunday drives' heyday, air conditioning was gaining momentum, but you'd be hard-pressed to find air-conditioned stores and homes in rural areas. Oh, you might see a window unit or two, but central air was rare. Breezes blew back windows' curtains and whirled through screen doors on sultry summer days. Inevitably, flies found their way inside and made themselves at home in the kitchen. It was there, at the hands of my grandmothers, that they met their maker.

Remember honest-to-goodness fly swatters made of screen-wire? My grandmothers wielded those instruments of doom with an Olympic fencer's skill. How many times did I watch those ladies pull off a trifecta: dispatching three flies with one swat.

My grandmothers didn't need bug sprays. Nor did they have newfangled bug zappers. No, they walked around with a screen-wire fly swatter in hand. While talking to me, their eyes would dart about, and a smooth backhanded "swat" sent Mr. Fly to that great compost pile in the sky. Those ladies had fighter pilot reflexes. They even clobbered flies buzzing in the air.

My grandmothers relied on the real deal. They would have disputed the *New Oxford American Dictionary*'s definition of *fly swatter* as "an implement used for swatting insects, typically a square of plastic mesh attached to a wire handle."

Plastic mesh? Please. Screen-wire swatters struck with deadly force and were far more effective than today's plastic swatters, which flies evade with ease. You see, the little critters detect changes in air pressure, and a clunky plastic swatter says, "Here I come" as its thick plastic air-mashing mesh tips off Mr. Fly. "I'm outta here," and off he buzzes. A thin mesh of screen-wire, however, arrives swiftly and silently with no shock wave, converting the fly to a countertop's version of roadkill possum.

Screen-wire swatters swat plastic swatters (say that seven times), but you will be hard-pressed to find a genuine screen-wire swatter today. All you'll find are plastic ones. Go online, however, and you can find honest-to-goodness screen-wire fly swatters. I suggest you get a few. Someday you will need them.

No visit to my grandmothers' homes was complete without watching those southern ladies reach for an old-fashioned screen-wire fly swatter. Both had radar. A flick of the wrist and a bloody stain marked the spot of the fly's demise. But now we have plastic swatters not worth a hoot. Flies live to drop specks yet again.

Know what else was good about screen-wire fly swatters? The vanquished fly stuck to the screen, where a shake over a toilet bowl buried the critter

Screen-wire swatters are the real deal. Don't waste your time on plastic swatters.

at sea. When a plastic swatter scores a kill over a slow, dimwitted fly, the departed remains right where it was, albeit wider, thinner, bloodier and, best of all, dead. But now you have to scrape up the mess.

One more thing: flies and kids make a bad combination. Kids have an annoying habit of standing in an open door, neither going in nor out. This will sound familiar to you baby boomers. "Close the door, you're letting flies in." Let 'em in we did, and when the flies flew inside, my grandmothers were armed and ready. The war commenced.

The days of smashing flies are behind us. Air conditioning made life more tolerable, but it robbed us of color, character and conflict. The war against flies required screen-wire swatters and cotton puffs stuffed in window screen holes. Despite such patchwork measures, pesky, nasty, greasy flies managed to invade the house. It was there that they encountered the original No Fly Zone, and if chaps, as we were called back in my day, got out of line, well, the swatter was good medicine for us too.

SEERSUCKER,
A SOUTHERN LEGEND

t's so damn hot I can't stand it. My fine seersucker suit is all soaking wet."
Texan Don Henley worked that seersucker reference into his song "The
Garden of Allah."

Seersucker. Just saying the word is pleasurable. The word sounds cool,
and cool is the operative word. In the days prior to air conditioning, a
southern gentleman worth his salt wouldn't be caught without a seersucker
suit. Back in the heyday of the Sunday drive, it was common to see southern
gentlemen in seersucker suits come Sundays. Atticus Finch wore it in the
sweltering courtroom in *To Kill a Mockingbird*.

How well I remember one gentleman back home in Lincolnton, Georgia,
Mr. Hughes Willingham, who wore seersucker pants in the dime store he
owned. I see him now. Wearing a white shirt and bow tie, with his hair slicked
back and those blue-and-white seersucker pants, he cut a stylish swath through
my memories. So did the best teacher who ever walked into a classroom. In
the spring of my freshman year at the University of Georgia, James Kilgo, in
a blue-and-white seersucker suit, read from William Faulkner's "The Bear,"
that classic story in *Go Down Moses*. As he read, white dogwood bracts swirled
by the windows of our classroom, an indelible image.

Seersucker reigns as a celebrity, and some celebrities loved this wondrous
fabric. Remember Andy Griffith and his seersucker suits with suspenders on
Matlock? Barney Fife would deck himself out in a seersucker suit topped off
with a straw hat and a bow tie when on the town. It was vogue, this fabric
once known as "the working man's suit," because of its affordability.

A seersucker suit is as southern as it gets.

Is seersucker southern to the core? You bet it is. The late Ken Burger, South Carolina writer and fellow UGA grad, had this to say about it: "Quite honestly, there's just something about wearing seersucker that makes you feel like you're starring in a James Dickey novel and talking to Mark Twain while having a drink with William Faulkner."

Sophia Loren, Ava Gardner and Suzy Parker wore it, and ladies, so can you. A woman told me, "Seersucker is my favorite thing to wear. I have a few seersucker dress suits from Brooks Brothers. Once I moved to Charleston, I realized it was a mandatory summer wardrobe item for surviving the oppressive heat of a blistering August day." She adds, "I have blue-and-white seersucker as well as tan and white, pink and white, etc. I love it all."

Seersucker comes from the Middle East, particularly Iran, and takes its name from the Persian words *shir-o-shakar*, which literally mean "milk and sugar." This was probably figuratively used, as the fabric is marked by both smooth and rough stripes, thus allowing the fabric to be held away from the skin, creating better air circulation.

From what I've learned, seersucker is made by slack-tension weave. The threads are wound onto the two warp beams in groups of ten to sixteen for a narrow stripe. The stripes are always in the warp direction and on-grain. Today, seersucker is produced by a limited number of manufacturers. It is a low-profit, high-cost item because of its slow weaving speed.

I can't wait for really blistering hot weather. I'll don a seersucker suit—blue and white, of course—and head to a book signing. And Henley, by the way, wasn't the only artist to weave seersucker into a song. The Rolling Stones' "West Coast Promo Man" talks about wearing a seersucker suit. The Tom Petty song "Down South" mentions seersucker and white linens, and The Who wrote "My jacket's gonna be cut and slim and checked, Maybe a touch of seersucker, with an open neck."

Seersucker—it was fitting apparel for Sunday church and many a Sunday drive. I see it more than I used to, so maybe it's making a comeback. Too bad it can't bring back the Sunday drive as well.

ALONG THE BORDER

Living at the edge of another state isn't bad. Just like that, you can be in another state. Nor is living along the Atlantic Ocean, though it limits where you can drive. Like the Georgia and North Carolina lines, the Atlantic makes for one of South Carolina's borders. Many of our Sunday drives were afternoon jaunts as well as extended drives into neighboring states.

DOWN HIGHWAY 64

I made a trip down memory lane across three states. When I got home six days later, the odometer registered 940 miles, with a foray to Hillsborough in the mix as well. On this journey from South Carolina into North Georgia and on into the Tarheel State, I made a major Sunday drive. I rolled up a good many of those miles driving down North Carolina's mountainous Highway 64.

My first goal was to retrace the route I'd traveled with my parents long ago. We'd take off early on a Sunday and head north to the hills. Get back well after dark. All these years later, I drove into Georgia to follow their trail. Loaded down with camera gear, water, coffee, luggage and an old-fashioned map, I struck out. The plan was to take Highway 76 up into South Carolina's northwest corner and cross the Chattooga into Georgia. Up around Dillard, Georgia, I would take Highway 23 into North Carolina, which would run me into Highway 64. There, I would turn east into the land of mountain memories, and ultimately, I'd visit an old racetrack.

THE CHATTOOGA

Highway 76 gets busy up near Anderson, South Carolina. It stays busy as it threads through Pendleton on up to and through Clemson, Seneca and on to Westminster. Once you near Long Creek, though, you are in apple orchard country, where the land pitches and heaves and a lot of cars and trucks carry kayaks.

At Long Creek, you'll see a strip mall designed to look like a town from the Old West. Among the buildings stand a post office, feed and hay store, hotel, U.S. federal bank, music hall, barbershop, newspaper stand and, a safe distance away, the jail. Consider this faux western outpost your last chance to get provisions such as ice cream before you come to the Chattooga River. I stopped there, and as I walked up to the colored façade of a store, two women came out. "I'm not sure what this is," one said to the other. "I think people will be disappointed," said the other.

I talked with the clerks about Woodall Shoals. "Lots of people on the river?" I asked. "Oh, yeah," said the woman loading a cone with two scoops of black cherry ice cream. After my ice cream, onward I drove to the Chattooga, a river that flows ten miles in North Carolina before carving a forty-mile watery border from the rock joining Georgia and South Carolina. The water running downhill here drops 2,469 feet over fifty miles (49.3 feet per mile), creating a legendary and strong-willed river.

There's no place to hitch your horse, but the ice cream is good.

The wild, scenic Chattooga looks like it did in the 1950s and the days of the Cherokee.

I have long had a love affair with the river that started before James Dickey's *Deliverance*. On one of our mountain forays in the 1960s, Dad drove us through a winding switchback road. We swayed to and fro with curves that slung the car around. Out of the corner of my eye, I spotted a wooden sign amidst dark green foliage in shadows: "Chattooga River." I saw no river and can only surmise to this day that we were far north of where the Chattooga foams and runs with fury. We had to be near where it was but a stream. Even so, my curiosity had been fired up. And later I read *Deliverance* and saw the movie. Fame for the river arrived.

Before that fame, before candy-colored kayaks arrived, mostly locals and whitewater enthusiasts knew about the river. For a dangerous while, a lot of amateurs challenged the river, often at the cost of their lives. The pilgrimage continues, and occasionally people die running the river. On my way in, I saw cars carrying kayaks, and when I parked at the Highway 76 visitors' center, I saw even more. Here near the comfort station you'll find a boulder with words carved into it: "Wild and Scenic Chattooga River May 10, 1974."

No matter when I visit the river, it has plenty to keep it company. On this particular journey, young men were leaping from rocks into the water below Bull Sluice. Then a whitewater running group arrived with their big raft attended by guides in kayaks. On a sandy shore within view of the 76 bridge, a couple enjoyed wine, cheese and grapes. The woman told me she was writing a novel. Isn't everybody?

What I love most about this river is its wild nature. It attracts romantics, and yes, it's dangerous and should never be taken lightly, but it is untamable and beautiful, and here you see nature's power at its best. Here, too, you see what happens when water, rocks and gravity take center stage in one of nature's most dramatic performances. Had I grown up nearer, I would have insisted that Dad take us on many a Sunday drive to the banks of the Chattooga.

SOJOURN 64

I made it to Highway 64, where I ran into an agreeable string of towns: Highlands, Cashiers ("cashers"), Brevard, Hendersonville, Bat Cave, Chimney Rock and Lake Lure.

Highlands sits in the Nantahala National Forest. Its average elevation of 4,100 feet will have you chewing gum to keep your ears from popping. It's cool and often rainy in Cashiers. Over eighty-five inches of annual rain keep those green hills green, except when snow blankets everything. Brevard, known for its white squirrels, sits in Transylvania County, and that dredges up images of vampires. Drive through the wooded hills here with appreciation. Consider the beautiful town the gateway to the Pisgah National Forest. Consider the area the birthplace of American forestry. The Cradle of Forestry (Biltmore Forest School), the site of the first school of forestry in the United States, operated during the late nineteenth and early twentieth centuries. Carl Schenk, a native German, taught at the school.

As you drive Highway 64 from Brevard toward Hendersonville, look for Oakdale Cemetery on your right. See the angel with outspread wings? It's the angel in Thomas Wolfe's *Look Homeward, Angel.* For years the angel stood on the porch of his father's tombstone shop in Asheville. You baby boomers will recognize the name Buffalo Bob Smith of *Howdy Doody* fame. He retired just south of Hendersonville.

Bat Cave, a community, takes its name from a nearby cave inhabited by several species of bats on Bluerock Mountain, the largest known granite fissure cave in North America.

Mom and Dad spent their honeymoon at Chimney Rock, a fact not lost on me when I checked into the Esmeralda Inn. *Esmeralda*. Is there a prettier word in the English language? (Frances Hodgson Burnett wrote the play *Esmerelda* [with an extra "e"] in 1881 while staying at an inn near Lake Lure, North Carolina.) If you are so inclined, walk the five hundred steps to the top of Chimney Rock for a seventy-five-mile view of the region.

Lake Lure has an interesting history as far as damming the Broad River goes. The Town of Lake Lure bought the dam and associated electricity generated. It sells power to Duke Energy. Hollywood likes the area. Films featuring scenes shot here include *Thunder Road*, *A Breed Apart*, *Firestarter*, *Dirty Dancing* and *My Fellow Americans*. Scenes in *The Last of the Mohicans* were shot at Chimney Rock and Hickory Nut Gorge.

Emerald-green hills and white cascades accompanied me on this nostalgic, literary and cinematic journey. And so did rocks. Lots of rocks. Massive boulders and sheer rock faces glistened here and there thanks to seeps, rivulets and waterfalls. I love it up here, so let me get this out of the way now. If you haven't been to this region in a long time, you're in for a shock. Development is ruining it. Places I recall tucked into woods stand exposed and surrounded by multitudes of businesses. This world could use a plague. Yeah, I said it.

The mountains serve up more surprises than the coast. The green crumpled hills confine your vision to what's in front of the windshield. Round a bend and the earth drops away. Round another curve and a waterfall thunders away. Climb a switchback highway and you drift in and out of clouds. Stand on a summer beach and you see, well, lots more beach and too many people.

Two places intrigued me on this journey. I wanted to see Carl Sandburg's writing office a second time, and I wanted to stay at the Esmeralda Inn.

Sandburg's home, Connemara, gives you good insight into how legends lived back in the day, but even here development has squeezed in close. You drive through suburbia to reach the parking lot. It wasn't that way sixteen years or so ago, and it sure wasn't like that when Sandburg's wife tended her beloved goats there. And what about that name, Connemara? That's a mouthful, isn't it. William Faulkner called his home Rowan Oak. Big-shot writers name their homes. Well, I have a name for mine too. I call it home.

Sandburg wanted a place to write, and he found it here in the Blue Ridge Mountains. Fate, chance, whatever you choose to call destiny's mingling of lives can make for strange bedfellows. The man who wrote a biography of Abraham Lincoln lived on the one-time estate of Christopher Memminger, the secretary of the Confederate treasury from 1861 to 1864.

Note the Remington Noiseless typewriter. It's heavy and solid, and one in good condition will fetch over $500.

In particular, I found Sandburg's writing space interesting. A National Park Service brochure photograph shows Sandburg at his typewriter in a cluttered office. The area that I photographed, however, looks spruced up. Well, perhaps the maid took care of things. Sandburg wrote on a Remington Noiseless typewriter. He had good company. Mark Twain was among the early users of Remington typewriters, and Rudyard Kipling used one as well. Margaret Mitchell used a Remington Portable No. 3 to write *Gone with the Wind*. Yes, the same Remington that produced firearms.

Colonel Tom Turner named the inn for the screenplay *Esmeralda* by Frances Hodges Burnett (author of *The Secret Garden*). The inn's location was once known as Esmeralda, North Carolina, since a post office was in the inn. Is it historic, this old inn? You decide. It's served as a stop for the Pony Express and stagecoaches and a hideaway for stars and a source of solitude and inspiration for novelists, playwrights and poets.

The Boy Scout Camp gym floor at Lake Lure now floors the Esmeralda Inn. The famous *Dirty Dancing* scene took place on it.

As for the Esmeralda Inn, I don't know that Mom and Dad honeymooned at the old Esmeralda Inn (it burned in 1917 and again in 1997), but I like to think they did. In the early 1900s, Hollywood fell in love with this region. The Esmeralda Inn served as a setting for many silent films. Maybe that's what attracted my parents to this place. Mary Pickford, Gloria Swanson, Douglas Fairbanks and Clark Gable stayed at the old inn. They found it to be a refuge, an escape from the crowds. Lew Wallace finished the script for *Ben Hur* in room 9. Many years later, Hollywood rediscovered the region, filming *Last of the Mohicans*, *Firestarter* and *Dirty Dancing* here.

Do you ladies recall the scene where Patrick Swayze and Jennifer Gray danced? I'm sure you do. Well, you walk that very floor now when you check into the Esmeralda Inn. I checked in and found it to be a beautiful, luxurious, quiet escape from the harassment of daily life. I stared at that floor recalling Otis Redding's voice, the "Mashed Potato" and other songs from *Dirty Dancing*. You can, too.

Nearby, the Broad River purls as it flows around huge rocks, and above it, a cliff brings to mind Yosemite's El Capitan. That's a bit of embroidery; nonetheless, it's a sheer face that looms over the Broad River and Lake Lure.

My Highway 64 sojourn. It gave me a chance to relive old memories and see where the poet who wrote *Abraham Lincoln, The Prairie Years* worked. Best of all, as the years slip by, my Sunday-like drive will stay in my mind, a reminder of family trips long ago, and always give me a chance to say that beautiful word, *Esmeralda*, to others here in the flatlands.

RACETRACK PHANTOMS

B ack in the 1960s, there were certain Sundays when making a Sunday drive was out of the question. Those were the Sundays Dad and I sat glued to the radio listening to NASCAR races. We pulled for the king, Richard Petty. We said not a word. Transfixed we were. Something about radio was more exciting than watching races on TV. Before men trained cameras on cars, I imagined colorful beads of speed strung around tracks. In my feverish mind, I could see long, lean, rounded tracks set into the land—paperclip-shaped ovals that fastened fame to speed. Then suddenly a tremendous clash as cars spun, tangled and burst into flames.

Somewhere along the track, I spun out. I lost my love for racing, but once I was a fan, and so, many years later, I made a Sunday drive to one of two tracks where it all began. My daughter, Beth, told me about an abandoned racetrack where people jogged and walked. I drove to the old Occoneechee Speedway up near Hillsborough, North Carolina, on July 5, a steamy Sunday threatening rain. The track's ghostly presence took me back to the Sundays Dad and I followed King Richard on the radio. How this horse track became a stock car track makes for a good story, a story every race fan should know.

Occoneechee. First it was a horse track. Then a man happened to fly over it and things changed. The South changed. The country changed.

***

In 1947, NASCAR's founder, Bill France Sr., was flying over Orange County, North Carolina, when he spotted a horse racetrack one General Julian Carr owned. France made the general an offer he couldn't refuse and prepared it for NASCAR's inaugural season in 1949.

France gave speed-hungry fans a way to see stock car races in the early 1950s near Hillsborough, North Carolina. Some watched for free. They could shimmy up a tree at the second turn of Occoneechee Speedway for a grand view of the .9-mile oval. Then the inevitable happened. Fireball Roberts lost control in turn two one day and smacked a tree. It was raining men, as the song goes.

Drivers loved Occoneechee. Most had never raced on a track bigger than half a mile. For all practical purposes, this .9-mile track was NASCAR's first super speedway. Over the next twenty years, legends in the making

Beth Shugg examines a car Herbert Cates drove. Cates, an Occoneechee phantom, was a local race car driver out of Hillsborough, North Carolina.

raced and wrecked here: Curtis Turner, Herb Thomas, Tim Flock, Joe Weatherly, Cotton Owens, Ned Jarrett, Bobby Allison, Bobby Isaac, David Pearson, Richard Petty and NASCAR's first superstar, Fireball Roberts. NASCAR was off and rolling.

Tens of thousands of fans came to Hillsborough over twenty years. It thrilled "Big Bill," as France was known, and he wanted to make Occoneechee into a track bigger than Daytona, but problems, minor and major, surfaced. Fans sneaked in without paying. Some climbed trees, as we've seen. Others slipped in across the Eno River. A problem bigger than freeloading fans, however, was brewing. Religion and racing made for a bad fit. One story goes that clergymen pressured local government to outlaw racing on Sundays. It's said, too, that the town of Hillsborough didn't like the reverberating roar of race cars. Another story holds that France wanted to build a super speedway here, but seven little church ladies fought France hard. Racing, they said, was too noisy for the Lord's Day. Little old ladies from Pasadena they weren't. Mostly it was local government's resistance to the idea of a big noisy track close by.

France told 'em that was all right. He'd give it a try in a place called Talladega. NASCAR grew into a huge sport, and Petty and other drivers became legends, setting the stage for big-time stock car racing. Maybe things worked out okay. "Hillsborough" doesn't sound like racing. "Talladega" does.

And Occoneechee?* Well, the last checkered flag dropped in 1968. That's when the Orange Speedway, Occoneechee's new name, saw its last race. Appropriately enough, the Hillsboro 150 was the forty-third race of the 1968 NASCAR Cup Series season, and it took place at Occoneechee Speedway on September 15, 1968. Richard Petty won it in his 1968 Plymouth, No. 43, from the pole with an average speed of 87.681 miles per hour. He outran twenty-three drivers. The King raced 150 miles, taking home $1,600 of the prize purse of $6,900. The track never roared again, and nature began to reclaim what had long been hers.

Decades later, "I was there," as the journalist used to say. Walking the back straightaway, I thought of all those Sundays listening to races with Dad. I stepped aside as ghostly drivers downshifted as they approached turns three and four. A tattered checkered flag flew for the King once again. In the blink of an eye, old race cars gave way to joggers, walkers and people walking dogs that pee and, well, you know.

---

* Occoneechee is one of three racetracks in the National Register of Historic Places.

Today, the track is eerily silent. Spirits sprint through the trees that overrun its dirt oval. A lot of time, a lot of changes, a lot of races have come and gone, and to me at least, NASCAR just isn't the same. Dad's gone, and I no longer follow NASCAR. The King retired long ago, and one Occoneechee driver's nickname proved eerily prophetic. Edward Glenn "Fireball" Roberts died on July 2, 1964, as a result of a fiery wreck at the World 600 in Charlotte. Dad and I heard about Roberts's accident on the radio, and I have no doubt we tuned in the races at Occoneechee. We heard legends roaring by thanks to Marconi's miracle, legends whose tracks I walked in one sultry Sunday, a day for remembrance and spirit chasing.

I sat on the cracked cement grandstand across from the finish line. It would have been a fine place where Dad and I would have seen Petty's electric-blue No. 43 take Occoneechee's last checkered flag. I sat there recalling Sundays listening to the radio with Dad. Once again, I imagined colorful beads of speed, this time strung around a tree-lined dirt track. Spectral cars and phantom drivers dodged trees, kicked up dirt, blasted the silence and hurtled past pines men once climbed. They raced and wrecked and wrecked and raced on this forgotten track that thrilled a father and son who sat with their ears glued to the radio. Long ago, we heard the roars and imagined the cars. What we couldn't imagine were seven church ladies and a rebellious local government that would have a hand in making Talladega, Talladega. Racing, they said, was too loud for the Lord's Day.

THE SOUTHERN STONEHENGE

You'll find an American Stonehenge standing on a rise just east of Highway 77 in Elbert County, Georgia, not far from the South Carolina border. The Georgia Guidestones, as they're called, stand on the highest point in Elbert County. A man using the pseudonym R.C. Christian hired Elberton Granite Finishing Company to build the structure. To this day, no one save one man, a banker, knows his real name, and the banker vows to take the secret to his grave.

Chiseled into the nearly twenty-foot-high granite slabs are admonitions for a future "Age of Reason." A CNN writer referred to Guidestones as "an astronomically complex, 120-ton relic of Cold War fears, built to instruct survivors of an Armageddon that the mystery man feared was all too near."

Read and go forth…
Maintain humanity under 500,000,000 in perpetual balance with nature.
Guide reproduction wisely—improving fitness and diversity.
Unite humanity with a living new language.
Rule passion—faith—tradition—and all things with tempered reason.
Protect people and nations with fair laws and just courts.
Let all nations rule internally resolving external disputes in a world court.
Avoid petty laws and useless officials.
Balance personal rights with social duties.
Prize truth—beauty—love—seeking harmony with the infinite.
Be not a cancer on the earth—Leave room for nature—Leave room for nature.

The Southern Stonehenge in Elberton, Georgia. Mystery attends these granite slabs. "Let these be guidestones to an Age of Reason."

Christian's ten principles are cut into the four vertical slabs, front and back, each side in a different language. Egyptian hieroglyphics, Babylonian cuneiform, Sanskrit and classical Greek inscribe the capstone.

A slot in the center column permits observation of the transit of the sun throughout the seasons. A hole higher up focuses on Polaris, the North Star. A hole in the capstone focuses a shaft of sunlight onto the central pillar at noon. These attributes let survivors of Christian's coming apocalypse reproduce the calendar, clock and compass—things a civilization must have. The Guidestones, by the way, attract controversy from critics who call them Satanic. Some call for them to be destroyed.

Blue granite. Mankind's big slate. Upon it we put all manner of messages. We build things with it. We make art with it and play football games within it. We make seats of government from it too.

There's something about this blue-white stone that I love. On my desk is a granite rock I commandeered from the watery clench of the Chattooga. It's been a lifelong love affair filled with joy and sadness, as love affairs are wont to be. Somewhere in the woods back home, my slingshot catapulted a million pieces of granite across the land. Perhaps some future archaeologist will unravel the mystery of how those bits of granite were strewn over the place. "A primitive weapon and amusement for boys," his learned paper will read.

Hard, durable and impervious, blue granite softens the hard edges of our lives. In it we find a record keeper. We remember our rock-slinging youth because of it. We memorialize fallen soldiers and lost causes with it. We prepare our meals on its surface. We lay our loved ones to rest with it, and we try, sometimes dramatically, to persuade mankind to live and act in accordance with injunctions and guidance.

When we see the quarries that birthed it, we should never forget the hard labor that wrests it free.

Blue granite, a stone from deep within the earth's bosom, makes for a place of eternal rest. Late one afternoon driving along a back road in North Carolina, I saw a grand angel of granite, wings outstretched in a small cemetery, overlooking an even smaller family plot framed in rusting wrought iron. Dogwoods bloomed, but their bracts had begun to fall…tears of alabaster, you might say. Spring was trailing away. Blue granite, however, is in season year-round. Blue granite, a rock of ages, is a stone you can't take for granted.

RUINS OF TABBY

Lowcountry folks itching for a Sunday drive have destinations like few others. Striped gray felines aside, that Spanish settler building concoction, tabby, never entered my childhood glossary. Why should it? Oysters were as removed from my life as were Spaniards, sand dollars and sea turtles. Years had to stack up before I would move to South Carolina and explore its Lowcountry. There I became conscious of tabby in a new way, and there I first heard that two-syllable term shot rapid-fire from transplanted lips.

A Yankee professor had to tell me about tabby. That rankles still. But forget that. How many real buildings does man cobble together from the remnants of meals? We're not talking gingerbread houses. We're talking enduring places that find their way onto historic lists. The kind photographers and artists love. The kind whose rough-textured ruins beg hands to touch them. Picturesque places at home among sawgrass, sand and Spanish moss.

When I see walls of ivory shells raised vertical from estuarine waters, I think of oysters as catering subcontractors. Long ago, men ate these bivalve mollusks, gaining sustenance, then applied that nourishment to the making of tabby and what would become ruins marinated in majesty. Steeped in a beautiful brine they were. That delectable architecture blesses us still. In yet another way, we are better off because of oysters.

So, what was the recipe for making that delectable building concoction? Men burned crushed oyster shells. That yielded lime, which they mixed with whole shells, sand and water in equal measures and poured into

This lighthouse stands behind a museum in the keeper's dwelling that chronicles coastal Georgia's history. The lighthouse and keeper's dwelling were completed in 1872.

forms. Lowcountry air then dried it. Dwellings that would stand the test of time resulted, and today's roll call of tabby structures is most distinguished. Men cast tabby blocks at Sapelo Island and then cast them into the sun to dry. Fort Pulaski's bricked underground bunkers, mortared strong with tabby, nonetheless fell to the Union. That beacon, the St. Simons Island lighthouse, rests on a tabby foundation. A tree, long dead, shores up a Wormsloe Plantation tabby wall. Imagine a fine sugary powder coating McIntosh Sugarworks oyster shells, and the Spring Island tabby remainders from Cotton King George Edwards's plantation are monumental in more ways than one. Jasper County has the White Hall Plantation House ruins and its tabby wings, and Beaufort has the Thomas Fuller House—the Tabby Manse—one of the few remaining early buildings on the South Carolina coast whose exterior walls are tabby entire.

This St. Helena Island landmark, built in the mid-1700s, succumbed to a forest fire in 1886.

Cumberland Island flaunts phantasmagorical ruins, the sprawling wreckage of Dungeness, a word as beautiful as tabby itself. Reading about tabby ruins is one thing. Seeing them is another. Come, walk with me beneath live oaks over and through the dappled shadows to St. Helena's Chapel of Ease. Rub your hands over its rough surface. Place your ear against that open shell stuck in the wall like no other. Child that you are, can you hear the sea? When sunlight strikes its walls just so, chapel shells shine like stars in the firmament. Now place your face against that pale, stone-like wall. Feel how sunlight soaks into shells…breathe in hints of alkaline.

Circa 1740, oyster banks sacrificed members of their dense aggregations to build a more convenient chapel for planters in and around St. Helena Island. In 1812, a parish church it became, and then the Civil War arrived only to be chased by abandonment. Methodist freedmen used the chapel until

130

a forest fire destroyed it in 1886. A conflagration banished the congregation, and the Chapel of Ease stands as you see it.

Friends, there are ruins and then there's ruination. In many places, oystering is a threatened way of life. Sewage spills. Overdevelopment. Water disputes. Too much rain. None of it does oysters any favors. Will the day come when tabby ruins stand as memorials to all we lost? I hope not. The Spanish brought tabby to St. Augustine circa 1580, and it came our way. Now, 438 years later, we have reason to worry. Nature's catering subcontractors gave us a delectable architecture. What can we give them in return?

GRAVES MOUNTAIN

On our Sunday drives, we often headed to places far different from where we lived. Often, that meant the mountains, but we had a mountain close by that we never visited. Though our mountain today is a ghost of itself, you can see it from afar, a lonely mountain, an outlier. When the tree line drops and the horizon opens up, there it stands, a mountain stranded by geology. Like so many things I remember from long ago, even this mountain submitted to change. Graves Mountain, it's called.

Just how did Lincoln County, Georgia, come to have a solitary mountain when the nearest mountain chain, the Blue Ridge Mountains, are about one hundred miles away up near Dillard, Georgia, and the North Carolina line? The answer is in an odd word: *monadnock*, an isolated small mountain that rises abruptly from a plain. Georgia's Stone Mountain is a monadnock. You could say a monadnock is a mountain in waiting.

Imagine an enormous rock deep within the earth covered by soil and softer rocks. As millennia pass, erosion sweeps away everything but the monadnock's harder, erosion-resistant rock, which rises as the surface washes away, like when hair falls out and a man goes bald.

We would drive by Graves Mountain, much higher then, and view it with awe. It was a place of legends such as the fable about a Cherokee maiden who leapt to her death when she was denied her true love. A mysterious cave and gold mine were said to exist there as well.

During the heyday of the Sunday drive, men began to mine this unique landmark. Massive explosions cleaved rock and caved away the mountain face. We can credit or blame geology for that. The mountain's original rocks were deposited about 300 million years ago. Then, during the continental collisions, the Lincoln County region was forced deep into Earth's mantle and subjected to heat and pressure. New minerals formed and existing minerals changed. Heat and pressure formed and re-formed different minerals until they metamorphosed into the erosion-resistant schists and quartzite. The dominant mineral emerging from this geologic cauldron was kyanite—a blue silicate mineral. Commercial mining began in 1963, and at one point, Graves Mountain produced half the kyanite in the United States. Much of that kyanite went into the ceramic material used in spark plugs. Is there a chance some of us drove around with Graves Mountain kyanite beneath our hood? I'd say there was.

An interesting thing happened on the way to mining all that kyanite for spark plugs and other uses. Graves Mountain became a coveted gem site. The blasting exposed rutile, a lustrous yellow gem, perhaps the mountain's most desired specimen. At one point during the extraction of kyanite, the mining company, American Silicates Inc., prohibited gem collecting. This didn't stop collectors, who, intent on getting specimens, got the word to mine workers. Equipment operators spotting a shiny rock would get down from their equipment to "relieve" themselves and grab the rock for an eager collector.

Today, gemstone collectors love Lincoln County rutile, and people all across the world know about Graves Mountain. Ask any rock hound where Georgia's most famous collecting site is. Your answer will be Lincoln County. The rutile, lazulite and pyrophyllite found here are among the finest in the world.

Of course, the geological community has long known about Graves Mountain. It was a famous mineral location in the 1800s, and that caught a lot of attention. None other than Tiffany's once owned Graves Mountain and its twin peaks, now blasted away. Back then, people called the mountain "Little Mountain."

When I was at the University of Georgia, my roommate Garnett Wallace and I were taking a geology course, and we went up to Graves Mountain nosing around. We figured we'd find some valuable rocks and make some cash. What we found was a steep climb, extreme heat and trouble. Climbing a sheer face, we got about halfway up but could go no farther. With great difficulty, we descended to safety. That was a long time ago, and what I remember most is how relieved we were to be on flat ground.

Growing up, I heard a lot of tales about Graves Mountain, fiction and fact. Helen Turner, my sixth-grade English teacher, told our class that the

Graves Mountain, Lincoln County, Georgia,
has some of the world's finest rutile, lazulite
and pyrophyllite.

ore being mined there would go into heat-resistant nose cones for rockets and missiles. That's a fact. The space race between the United States and the Soviet Union was heating up, and it excited me to think that my home would contribute to the exploration of outer space. Now man has walked on the moon and the space race is over.

Today when I drive Highway 378 past Graves Mountain, I imagine it before mining blasted away its top. I recall when a Sunday drive took us past it on our way to the North Georgia mountains. It stood several hundred feet taller. There, in the "real" mountains, we saw swift, cold, stone-studded streams laden with gemstones, or so we were told. Years later at "mountain mines," I'd buy bags of dirt that my daughters sifted in a sluice. They'd pour dirt into a screen box and hold it in the sluice, looking for gemstones, salted, of course. The real gem, however, was back home—the mountain of my youth.

And what's behind the name "Graves Mountain"? Well, there was no cemetery on the flanks of that lonely mountain. I never heard of a grave there. The mountain came by its name thanks to "Old Man Graves," a fellow who once upon a time owned what would become a world-famous site for collecting gems. The old-timer owned a place we passed on Sunday drives where visions of a Cherokee maiden plunging to her death came to mind. Dark hair streaming like some failed parachute, she crashed onto the rocks below.

It loomed large, too, as a mysterious place crawling with rattlesnakes, but looking back, I don't believe rattlers would prefer that habitat, so that might have been nothing more than a story to scare away curiosity seekers. Maybe Old Man Graves gave rise to that myth. There's no doubting, however, what gave rise to Graves Mountain—ancient geological processes in the deep bowels of Mother Earth—and many a Sunday we passed it by for the mountains of North Georgia and North Carolina.

MOM'S PEACH TREE ORPHAN

A date tree grew in my grandmother's backyard. The taste was dry and bittersweet. Grandmom had crabapples too. Sour. All the old folks planted fruit trees. Pear, apple, cherry, wild plum and peach trees. Pecan trees too. Wild grape vineyards—scuppernongs and muscadines. Folks in general don't do that anymore. Oh, they plant ornamental fruit trees that bear no fruit, such as the Bradford pear (a tree scorned more and more), but when it's time for fruit, they go to the store and buy fruit that's waxed and arranged in pretty rows. Well, it wasn't always that way.

From my mental map of Sunday drives rises one lonely peach tree, an orphan. I see it now. Stunted, short, lean and green, with tiny peaches. My parents planted it. All these years later, I know right where it stood, near the wood's edge in front of our home. Try as I might, I cannot see it in bloom, but I remember its peaches. Not much bigger than their pits, stunted.

Somewhere down the line, that tree died of loneliness, bereft of an orchard to comfort it, to show how regal it looked. If a tree can suffer a broken heart, that one did. Memories of it live on, and that tree was on my mind when I trekked into Edgefield County one chilly March morning. I got up at 5:15 a.m., threw on the coffee, made ready to leave and arrived in peach country just after sunrise. A heavenly sight waited: clouds of pink, pale red and coral, a blushing performance of mesmerizing delicate blooms. That afternoon, as I was packing up my camera gear just off Highway 19, three women pulled in. They rushed over to a tree, posed and began snapping photos.

"We're from Florida. We never see anything like this," said a dark-haired girl. Their tag verified they were, indeed, from Yankee South. Well, they have orange groves, but a woman down Florida way tells me orange trees aren't as spectacular as peach trees, though they're fabulously fragrant. As I drove off, the women were giggling and hopping around, snapping photo after photo. High on peach trees they were.

Mom and Dad were high on them too. Early in spring, they would cross the border into peach country to scout out the orchards. I imagine that one lonely peach tree had to be beautiful. Well, hundreds and hundreds of them are like a soft pink mantle fallen to earth.

Once spring had given way to summer, my parents looked forward to a ritual: driving to Edgefield County to buy peaches. Down Highway 378 across the Savannah they drove, taking a right onto Highway 28 in McCormick and a left onto Highway 283 in Plum Branch. Plum tickled they were. Across Stevens Creek they went and on to Highway 25 into Edgefield proper on through the square to its peach orchards. Back home, they returned with split-oak baskets overflowing with sweetness. It wasn't long before peach pies, fresh sliced peaches, pickled peaches and homemade peach ice cream blessed family gatherings.

Knowing how Mom loved flowers, I'm sure the drive to peach country provided double joy—good things to eat and profuse blooms with few equals. Along the way, I'm sure they talked about growing up with fruit trees. The seed was in their blood. At Granddad Poland's farm, a pear tree, heavy with fruit, stood by a barn. I saw my only butchering of a cow at that barn. Once was enough. That pear tree? I'm going to look for it one day, and if it's there, I'll photograph it, but there's no going back to photograph Mom's lonely peach tree. There's no going back to photograph Mom and Dad.

Well, things change, don't they? From now on, come spring I'll photograph Edgefield County's blushing crowns. As winter fades, I'll keep an eye on the blooms' progress. When conditions seem close to perfect, I'll make a modern-day Sunday drive into peach country. It's something to do—something to look forward to, something to remember, like Mom's broken-hearted peach tree. But its beautiful petals, delicate blossoms that surely drifted across our yard like pink snowflakes? For the life of me, I just can't summon them up.

Peach orchards in Edgefield, South Carolina, bless the land with unparalleled color and beauty early in March.

TIME PASSAGES

All the years did go by, and they brought wholesale change with them. I regret all the times I wished to be all grown up. I wished away some special times. What was I thinking? Well, the land and our society grew up, too. Sometimes when I reflect on my life, I see myself as a stranger. I am not who I once was. I feel the same way about life today. It's different and heavily populated by strangers and strange ways. Every generation feels its ways were the best, but my generation has lived through a lot of change, and they say experience is the master teacher. I'll go with that.

DREAMS OF HUNTING

Woods and fields pulled on me hard when I was a boy. I grew up on the edge of a large hardwood forest, and I rambled in woods every chance I got. I saw deer, wild turkey, ducks and occasionally I'd walk up a covey of quail. When they flushed, it sounded like a bomb going off.

In the early 1960s, I read *Outdoor Life*, cover to cover. In it, Lowcountry plantations hosted duck, deer and quail hunts. I saw such places as romantic adventures, and I was eager to wear fine hunting apparel and own exquisite firearms. Freezing in a duck blind? That was for me. Birds on the wing? Count me in. Outwitting a magnificent whitetail buck? That was the epitome, except for two problems: no one taught me anything about hunting, and the only gun I had was a Mossberg .410. But I dreamed on, fantasizing about icy mornings, the fragrance of leather and gunpowder, the click of the safety and recoil of Winchesters and Remingtons.

The best I could do was to shoot squirrels, but during many an autumn Sunday drive, I was quick to spot a deer stand, a field edge haunted by quail and a brace of mallards soaring over a pond or lake. Daydreams of hunting filled quiet moments on our Sunday drives, but the day would come when my deer hunting fantasy would turn real.

I landed a job as a scriptwriter for natural history documentaries at South Carolina Wildlife (SC DNR), and my job required me to take part in a Lowcountry deer hunt. The boss of bosses, John Culler, also a Georgian, believed that writers must experience what they write about. For a Georgia boy whose hunting résumé read "Squirrels Only," I was stepping in high cotton, but at last I would see a Lowcountry plantation and have the chance to shoot a deer. Maybe. The reality was I had become a man who loved words, and the hunt now was to better understand myself.

The place of high cotton, Bonneau Ferry Plantation, an old plantation once known as Prioli, sat on the Cooper River's eastern branch. The sprawling site harbored an eighteenth-century plantation house and ruins. One such ruin is Strawberry Chapel, a chapel of ease built around 1700—the last remaining building of Childsburg, a bustling town until the Civil War came along.

Westvaco owned Bonneau, and each year it put on the dog for the media, the centerpiece of which was an autumn deer hunt. Blue jean me? I was sent to get an education.

We departed Columbia on an October afternoon, when sunlight rains down like golden honey, blue shadows steal across highways and Spanish moss wears a crown of light. Arriving a bit after five o'clock, we entered the plantation through twin ranks of live oaks drenched with just such Spanish moss. Here came black gentlemen in tuxedos holding silver trays laden with cocktails and cigars. Out back, men shot clay pigeons along the banks of the Cooper, shells flying, discharges reverberating o'er rice fields. The sun was dropping. The air had a chill. Hearts filled with joie de vivre. Men were living a dream.

Our host, Westvaco's Coy Johnston, welcomed us and laid out the rules for the morning hunt. "It's advisable," he said, "to harvest [kill] smaller bucks with unattractive racks."

I had never killed a deer, and that evening I considered that weighty act. "Somewhere in those deep, green woods," I thought, "an animal may be living its last night because I am dispatched to these river woods."

With butterflies in my stomach, I made the rounds, shaking hands. The fragrance of fine cigars drifted throughout the well-appointed house. That and the camaraderie of outdoorsmen and writers evoked the kind of life Ernest Hemingway must have lived. Two words drifted through the blue smoke, drifting against paneled walls: "rustic opulence." Many years later, a chance encounter with a fellow who had been there that night remembered what I remembered. "You could open any cabinet in the house," he said, "and it would be full of all kinds of brands of liquor, cigarettes and cigars."

For dinner, we had steaks as big as cedar planks. After dinner, billiards, poker, adult beverages, blue smoke and wild stories filled the long evening. I retired around 1:30 a.m., knowing I had to rise at 4:30 for breakfast before being driven to a deer stand.

In pre-dawn darkness, the energizing, fragrant aroma of coffee lured me into the breakfast room. Black cooks in white aprons brandished cast-iron skillets as big as snowshoes. Breakfast was a feast of eggs, bacon, steak, grits, biscuits and steaming coffee. After breakfast, I boarded a pickup full of authentic hunters, and the truck dropped me off at my stand, which looked like the Tower of Babel. Up I went, pulling a borrowed and for sure empty 30.06 behind me on a rope.

I wore no camouflage, just jeans and a work shirt. Loading my rifle, I reminded myself that I was given no choice but to hunt. "Well, I don't have to shoot a deer," I said to myself. "Didn't see a damn thing." That'd be my story. Still, I wondered, could I pull the trigger? I recalled that a writer long ago wrote some powerful words: "A man needs to know if he can kill something or somebody." Hemingway? Perhaps.

The east lightened. A flock of wild turkeys passed beneath my stand, and after an interlude of birdsong, a patch of brush seemed to move, a gray-brown illusion. I thought my eyes were fooling me, but it was an apparition turning real. Materializing like a spirit, a buck with a small, asymmetrical rack came down the trail. On he came, closer and closer. "Go away," I thought, "go away." On he came. The gun was in my hand, my finger on the safety. I had a decision to make. Should I shoot this animal? The rule concerning unattractive racks said, "You must."

I raised the barrel and clicked the safety off. One shot to the heart dispatched the animal, a merciful killing, thank God. Back at the plantation house, I watched two men hang the deer from an oak limb's dangling chain and dress the deer precisely, like surgeons.

* * *

That was in another lifetime. So much has changed since then, and I, for certain, have changed. Hunting, it turns out, was not my life calling. I didn't feel good about what I had done. The mind, however, never lets us forget some things. Sometimes memories of Bonneau Plantation come to me when I see oaks covered with resurrection ferns and Spanish moss. Sometimes they come when I smell bacon and coffee on an early fall morn. They always come when I see a chain hanging from an oak.

Bonneau Ferry. It was the only time I hunted deer, but I left that place carrying something. A glimpse of what I knew were glory days down South, the days of bourbon, camaraderie, gallantry, good food and one other thing—the knowledge that, yes, I was capable of handing out death. Once.

Something I never got to do back in those Georgia hardwoods of home, and something I was glad I didn't, as it turned out.

Bonneau Ferry had, indeed, ferried me back, back to and beyond my boyhood days of reading *Outdoor Life* and daydreaming of deer hunts as Dad's two-tone Plymouth skirted woods and fields. Part of my life journey was complete, and I knew myself a bit better.

BAPTIZED IN A CREEK

Mom and Dad did their best to raise me right. That meant going to church each Sunday. Dressed properly, we'd get into Dad's two-tone Plymouth and make the five-minute drive to New Hope Baptist Church. We'd go to Sunday school, then preaching and afterward have Sunday dinner. Then, if the stars aligned, we'd make a Sunday drive, during which we passed many a church.

I thought a lot about religion in my youth. Everyone I knew went to church, and our small county seemed to have more churches than stores, which I believe is a fact still. But those Sunday drives taught me something: every county had lots of churches, and to me that meant lots of baptisms.

Here's how I joined the church. I was sitting on a pew between two Roberts, my cousin Robert Steed and Robert Williams. I was twelve years old. When the preacher called for salvation, the piano and choir took up "The Old Rugged Cross." Just then, both Roberts stood up and walked down to the pulpit. After a minute, not to be left alone, I joined them. Our baptism was primitive, as you'll see, but for now flash-forward decades.

I was down home visiting my family for Easter, and we went to our church. As I sat listening to a special music program, it was hard not to stare at the baptismal pool behind the choir. As hard as I try to accept that pool, I cannot. While staring at it, my thoughts turned to three pivotal days in a church we never forget: the day we accept Christ, the day we're baptized and the day we lay a loved one to rest.

No matter what people do today, you can be sure they want to do it as conveniently and comfortably as possible. When I say everything, I mean everything. I present to you a modern-day convenience that killed the days of baptizing souls in a river or creek in the woods: the baptismal pool inside the church. These ultra-clean fiberglass pools are charming. Through their clear walls, you see the Holy water, we'll call it. Above the pool, an idyllic scene from the Holy Land greets you. No longer do you have to walk to a creek. You don't have to worry about frogs and snakes, and you can make the water as warm as bathwater. Moreover, you can save folks' souls any season now because cold weather is no big deal. But it wasn't that way when I was a twelve-year-old boy.

It was the August Revival of 1961 when I walked to the pulpit to accept Christ. Back then, when enough people had professed their desire to wash their sins away, a baptizing ceremony went on the calendar. When that day arrived, folks would wear Sunday clothes but bring a change of clothes for the ceremony. They'd cross Highway 220 to a bit of woods where a pretty good creek ran. Straddling that creek was a shack fronted by a small concrete creek-fed pool. They changed clothes in that old wood shack. A sheet with a hole cut into it made a cape that folks pulled over a T-shirt and slacks or blouse and dress. Then they sat and waited their turn to be dipped. At the pool's shack end were steps. The preacher and his soon-to-be new members would descend these steps into the pool as the moment approached.

Our time for baptizing was in the dead of winter, a cold day when your breath looked like a drag off a Chesterfield. Upstream, men were heating fifty-five-gallon drums of water over a fire. When the water got really hot, they'd dump it into the stream. A deacon would test the water and signal the preacher when warm water was on the way. Downstream, another deacon would test it also. I waded in behind the Reverend Edwin Dacus, who slipped me beneath the tepid water. It was a cold introduction to the Lord.

That Easter Sunday I visited my family, I went back to the creek and its sad little pool. What better time to visit the spot where you were baptized than Easter Sunday. For the first time in decades, I visited that place important in my personal history. It had changed beyond belief. The creek was dried up, and the little shack where we waited our turn to be baptized was falling down. The little concrete block–lined pool was intact and filled with water. Everything was grown over with briars, bushes and tangled undergrowth. Slowly, my memories returned, and I remembered a place nowhere as sterile as the baptismal pool inside my church. That old creek-fed pool had character. It was part of nature, real and appropriate.

Somehow the image of John the Baptist dipping Jesus in a super-clean baptismal pool just doesn't hold up to classic paintings of John taking Jesus beneath the Jordan River. But hey now, we have yet another modern way to replace time-honored traditions—the fiberglass, chlorinated baptismal pool.

Selling these modern baptismal pools relies on getting the word out to churches and their leaders. Consider this marketing message for fiberglass baptismal pools: "Having a baptistery as a permanent fixture of a church adds beauty, character, as well as convenience, allowing your church the privilege of being able to baptize all throughout the year. The presence of one of our baptisteries makes the busy life of a minister a lot easier, wasting no time wondering where the next baptism will take place."

Something about that advertisement seems phony. Nothing phony, however, attended my old baptismal pool—alas, a dying custom. The place where I was baptized is succumbing to time, gravity and the elements. Even the creek has narrowed to not much more than a rivulet. Erosion, sedimentation and plant succession fills it in. That's a shame. A lot of souls were saved there.

As for old-time baptisms, we can say what's often said when an unforgettable fellow passes on: "We won't see the likes of him again." That old baptismal pool in the woods has sat unused for maybe sixty years now. No, we won't see the likes of it again.

I don't know if our government has passed some law forbidding baptismal rites in honest-to-goodness creeks, rivers or lakes, but it wouldn't surprise me. We're all about protecting people from every conceivable calamity these days. God forbid some child gets a leech stuck to his snoot at the precise moment his sins wash downstream.

The old-time baptism in a creek was good enough for generations, and it was good enough for me. Time marches on. Now it's robbed us of another memorable practice: the country rite of baptizing souls as Jesus was baptized.

Ceremonies in a fiberglass pool? They all look unremarkably the same, are quite comfortable and lack drama.

DINNER ON THE GROUNDS

Sunday drives took us by many a church where I'd see cedars, a cross, a cemetery and long tables made from concrete and stone. I remember homecomings long ago at my church, New Hope. People filled the sanctuary, Dr. Cutts preached a tad long and ladies' funeral home fans shooed away wasps. After all the soul saving ended, folks visited in the sanctuary. Homecoming was a kind of reunion, and while the old folks caught up, I skedaddled outside, where the main event would take place: dinner on the grounds.

Back then, we stood and ate at two long "tables" made from concrete blocks topped by stone slabs. Shaded by several large cedars (cut and gone), those primitive tables served their purpose just fine. Church ladies draped white tablecloths across them, and upon those tablecloths sat a southern cookbook of fine eating. We dined like kings, queens, princes and princesses.

For certain, I look back on dinner on the grounds with more fondness than I do social gatherings in the fellowship hall. Yes, flies flitted about those old tables and it was hot, but it should have been hot, a reminder of where we'd end up if we didn't toe the line, and that would be with the "Debil."

Many times I've wished those old tables still stood to the right of that white church with its tin roof. Tables like those of my youth gave way to progress, I assumed, and I'd never see their kind again. Wrong. One July day, I spotted Little Stevens Creek Baptist Church down a long driveway off Highway 430 in Edgefield County, South Carolina. Storm clouds filled the sky and a dark line of woods provided a backdrop to the church. Its bright white architecture pulled me down that long entrance, where a wonderful surprise waited.

Behind the church stood two stone and cement tables like I remembered from New Hope. A flood of memories came at once. Yellow-and-white dishes mounded over with potato salad, blue-and-white CorningWare filled with casseroles, platters of fried chicken, string beans, sliced tomatoes, rolls, cornbread, squash and loaves of what Granddad Poland called "white bread." All manner of cakes and pies and jugs and jars of iced tea. Folks heaped food onto plates known as Melmac. Try as I might, I just cannot recall Styrofoam cups and plates back in the days of "cement" tables, nor do I remember plastic milk jugs of tea. I recall china plates, stainless steel flatware, Tupperware and possibly some paper plates. We didn't have such an artificial world back then. Dinner on the grounds was a tradition, and the word that describes dinner on the grounds for me? "Real."

Before "fellowship halls" came along, people ate on cement tables. These tables belong to Little Stevens Creek Baptist Church, Edgefield County, South Carolina.

I remember the food more so than the people, but I can see Mom there in her stylish dark hair and 1960s glasses showing me where her food was. (I was a tad reluctant to eat other folks' cooking, but I got over that foolishness with time.)

Dinner on the grounds made memories for a lot of us. Said Lincolnton, Georgia native Sheila Poss Callahan, "I loved those outdoor tables. When I was a little girl, Daddy [Thomas Poss] and Granddaddy [Arlin Walker] would lift me up onto the tables at Midway Church and let me run the entire length and jump into their arms. It was like flying!"

Reesie Poss remembers, "As a child those tables at Martins Crossroads seemed to be one thousand feet long. They were endless, and full of all the best food on Homecoming Sunday. Such fond memories."

Daryl Bentley recalls the tea: "There's nothing like the flavor of church picnic sweet tea. I've finally come to the conclusion that it's because so many different versions were stirred together."

And I remember long stone tables beneath vanquished cedars. We dined in sunlight, not fluorescent light. Ants appreciated the crumbs that fell from heaven. There were flies, but there were breezes too. Ice chests dispensed ice, not modern refrigerators, and the ice seemed colder, the tea sweeter.

Dinner on the grounds stood tall in a place called Memory. The new fellowship halls with their wheelchair ramps and air conditioning are good for the aged and infirmed. No doubting that, but wedding receptions, funeral meals and homecoming dinners blur into indistinguishable events, for me at least. The surroundings just seem too much like restaurants. I doubt kids today will grow up with memories of fellowship halls, but I bet they'd remember eating outside off long stone slabs as a business of flies pestered them. Gnats, too.

Make a Sunday drive today and you'll rarely see old cement-stone tables. You'll see a fellowship hall. Often its architecture is out of step with the church's, but it's not out of step with the times. To have a fellowship hall is a trendy thing. Well, it wasn't always this way. Those of us who ate on rock slabs fanning flies away might sound like primitives, but we're blessed with memories, and there's no doubting that.

COTTON FIELDS
AND SEWING MACHINES

On Sunday drives, we couldn't avoid farm country. It surrounded us, and sometimes we passed a field of cotton filled with snow-white bolls. Mom paid attention to those fields. When she was a girl, she picked cotton, toting a big sack to put it in. A lot of cotton. On our drives, however, big machines sat idle, waiting to pick it. Sometimes red, sometimes green, big machines made by McCormick and International Harvester had replaced hand pickers.

When autumn sunlight struck a field of cotton, the cotton was whiter than white, and those cotton fields set Mom to recalling the old days, the days when women used Singer sewing machines to turn cotton into dresses. She had good recall of her dad's farming and shared her memories with me. In the truly old days of farming, folks made things we'd consider odd today, dependent as we are on mass-produced machines. Necessity was indeed the mother of invention. Take, for instance, a stick festooned with strips of old newspaper. That would be a shoofly stick, waved over the dinner table to keep flies and gnats away. Back in more primitive times, other simple inventions made life easier for farmers and their families. A cider press. A cotton seed cleaner. A colic medicine dispenser for mules and horses. All manner of iron plows and tool. Pie safes, which usually had their legs cut off for a simple reason. The legs rotted away because each leg stood in a jar lid filled with water to keep ants out of the pies.

The essentials and trappings of farm life long ago included things such as a butter churn, pressing irons, a wooden scooter plow and an old seeder cleaner. That cleaner let one man clean the same amount of seeds fifty men could clean by hand in a day. Much of what farmers grew ended up on their table, and their self-sufficiency included clothes made of cotton. A sewing machine was a vital piece of equipment, something I appreciated as a fashion-conscious teenager. Back around 1965, a fashion craze swept through high school. Cranberry button-down shirts emerged as *the* shirt to have, and like other young bucks, I had to have one. Nothing's worse than being a teenager out of step with fashion. When it became apparent my folks weren't getting me a store-bought shirt, Grandmom Poland said she would make me one, and she did. Made it on her Singer sewing machine. The collar was a bit out of line and the buttonholes a tad large, but I loved that shirt and plumb wore it out.

Remember sewing? It used to be part of family life, and there was a time when women bought bolts of cloth and made clothes for the family. It doesn't seem that long ago that I watched Grandmom Poland pump the treadle and make that Singer sing. The song would start slowly, but pressure on the treadle would rev it up, and that machine would hum right along. I recall sewing's rhythmic tune, seeing parchment-like paper etched with faint blue patterns and hearing words like rickrack, facing and gathering. I recall, too, the complex act of threading the machine and seeing all manner of machine accessories. A wooden spool of thread sat on a pin, and adjusting the thread tension proved critical. Sewing seemed mechanical and magical, but more than anything, it seemed to be a labor of love.

I hope I told Grandmom how much I appreciated the shirt she made me because it must have taken days to make. And that brings me to a question: do young women sew today? Do they pin patterns to cloth and cut fabric with the utmost care? Do they lovingly put an old Singer sewing machine to work and hear it sing its song?

My guess is they don't. It takes too much time, and so old Singers sit idle. They collect dust like the ones here that I photographed in Carlton, Georgia. And besides, just why should a young woman sew today? Plenty of stores sell clothes in a dizzying array of styles and sizes. There was a time, though, when you had to make them yourself, and there used to be a high school course called home economics where girls learned sewing and other practical skills, but those days are out of fashion now. Change marches on, but even I learned to appreciate sewing's practical side. Granddad Poland wore overalls. He was short, and Grandmom would shorten new overalls' legs and hem them to fit. She'd sew the end of a discarded leg piece together, sew on a strap and just like that I had a granite pebble bag for my slingshot.

Gilded and ornate, a Singer sewing machine is a work of art. A Sunday drive turned up these beauties in Carlton, Georgia.

From that bag grew my love for camera bags, Pony Express–type bags and leather luggage.

No, I doubt young women sew today, and I'll admit that today's husbands and beaus should be thankful they don't. Few things are more painful for a man than being dragged through cloth world. A trip to cloth world 'twas a fate worse than death. And when I was a boy, few things made me happier than that cranberry button-down collared shirt I wore in high school. Grandmom sewed it, and it marked the beginning of my love affair with fashion, Brooks Brothers, seersucker suits, bow ties, jackets, sweaters and more.

When I see a cotton field, I think of an old letter one of Mom's aunts wrote about picking cotton at night beneath a full moon. I have yet to see moonlight bathe a cotton field with silver light, yet to see thousands of silver-gilt cotton puffs glow with unworldly brilliance, but it's on my list of things to do.

Today, when a drive takes me by a cotton field, I think of a girl picking those white bolls. That would be my mom. And whenever I see an old Singer sewing machine, which is rare, I think of Grandmom sewing that cranberry shirt for me. It wasn't store bought, but it was made with love and fit just fine.

Homemade clothes are passé, and we're that much more dependent on some seamstress we'll never meet, someone, no doubt, in another country. Like a seam-ripper, change guts us of yet another custom, and old Singer sewing machines sing a tune nowhere as common as it once was.

Or so I thought. Several ladies in sewing clubs convinced me that the old Singer sewing machines still sing their song. Not all of the old ways are dying out. Cotton still goes from the fields and threads its way to sewing machines. The old pedal-operated machines still sing their song, but young girls picking cotton? You won't see that.

AN OLD CHAIN GANG CAMP

T hat's the sound of the men working on the chain ga-a-ang." Sam Cooke sang that, and Chrissie Hynde and the Pretenders had a take on chain gangs, too. I have no memories of seeing chain gangs working roadsides, but they did. Dad remembered hearing his father, born in 1903, talk about chain gangs.

In the early 1900s, drivers often saw prisoners working on highways. Chained together at the ankles, they'd dig ditches, build roads and perform other forms of hard labor. Many people compared this penal system punishment to slavery, as most prisoners were black. Penal reform arrived in the 1940s, and chain gangs began to be less common. By the mid-1950s, drivers no longer saw chain gangs working the roads of the South. Today, however, it's not unusual to see orange prison togs on jailed and imprisoned people picking up litter along highways. Call it roadside beautification. The backbreaking old chain gangs of yore are gone, but if you make a drive one Sunday down Highway 25 into Edgefield, South Carolina, you can see a relic of the chain gang years: a chain gang camp. A Sunday drive to this camp takes you back to a time in history when it was common to see men working along and on highways.

The chain gang camp building itself was built in the 1930s. The area around the building served as a cemetery before the camp was built. Most graves bear no markers, just numbers. Ten women photographers and I traveled there on a brutally hot, brutally humid day. My white linen shirt clung to me like saran wrap. Not the best day for going afield, but that was

Highway 25, Edgefield County, South Carolina. Inside, a metal cot waits for weary souls who no longer toil.

the plan. Ten women and I set out beneath a searing sun to explore western South Carolina.

We convened at the Park and Ride at Exit 5 off I-20. Photographer Cherrie Alexander arrived driving a black Ford Transit van, and we loaded our gear and piled in. Down Highway 25 we went to the historic Edgefield Square. We headed out again, and just outside Edgefield, photographer Pam Cook told us about the old chain gang camp. We parked and waded through Queen Anne's lace and knee-high, sometimes waist-high grass to photograph the main building, built in the 1930s with granite commandeered from the old Edgefield jail. The area around the building had been a burial ground before the camp came to be. It's been used as a burial site as late as the 1990s, with most graves unmarked and overgrown. Photographer Holly Bartley came across the grave of Freddie Williams, but we were unable to learn more about Williams.

An old butcher knife lay in a window crisscrossed with rust-speckled bars, the proverbial crossbars hotel. That ominous touch, like a prop in an old movie, seemed right. An austere metal cot in a room with cracked green plaster had long accommodated exhausted souls. Holly photographed a stout metal ring fastened to the floor, possibly a way to chain the gang inside the old building. As for the building itself, its step-like façade dredged up a Clint Eastwood western, like some waystation in *The Good, the Bad and the Ugly*.

You could feel the presence of ghosts. Fists gripped the rust-flecked steel bars. Cots squeaked and chains rattled. And that old butcher knife was troubling. Just why was it there after all these years? Funny thing, too, about the tall grass in front of the building. When bursts of wind ghosted over and through it, I could easily imagine chained men walking through. I didn't venture out back to see the graves. Maybe someday I will.

Now and then when I go to Edgefield down Highway 25, I stop at the old camp and check it out. You can too. A historic place like this old camp makes for a good Sunday drive destination. Here, you see firsthand a vestige of days long past, the place where weary chain gang prisoners rested and died. Look for the graves behind the old camp building. And today when you must drive along one of our boring interstates and see orange-clad prisoners, note that they are not chained together. They're doing a line dance called "Highway Beautification."

HOMEMADE MUSEUMS

Many vintage sights and settings that made Sunday drives special disappeared. Kudzu dragged down classic homes, rust corroded nostalgic signs, old gas pumps stand empty and rock piers reveal where country stores burned. Now and then, though, you'll pass through a time warp. Around a bend, at the end of a straightaway, at the edge of a field, on a city street, even, stands an old gas station, post office or store turned museum. All of a sudden, you're years in the past. You'll pass a farm where the owner has assembled old tractors and implements from many years back. You'll come across a lot of classic cars, restored like new—brilliant chrome, classic lines and fabulous colors.

Coming across a countryside museum is to discover a chest of treasure. In one spot, a self-appointed curator has stockpiled bygone years. Time preservers, these men and women hang onto sights once common in the days of Sunday drives, and in doing so, they conserve the past.

HIGHWAY 101

Travel Highway 101 in upper South Carolina and you'll pass a country store not far from Hickory Tavern. This blast from the past makes it easy to imagine you're on a Sunday drive in the 1950s. On the store's right side are five reminders of days past, including an icon of the South: the revered RC Cola/Moonpie combination, the workingman's lunch. One ad is real, but the others are painted onto the store's boards. From afar, that's hard to discern.

Coca-Cola has done its part to give us memorable images over the years, and a pretty woman on a diving board doesn't diminish that legacy. In its early days, sign artists painted Red Man Chewing Tobacco ads on the sides of barns, often with an endorsement from baseball player Nap Lajoie: "Lajoie chews Red Man, ask him if he don't."

The building's front pairs Lucky Strike cigarettes with Orange Crush. Lucky Strike came out in 1871 and took its name from the era's gold prospectors. Peer through the windows into the past. Vines have invaded the place. Nature reclaims whatever she can.

The store's left side has ads that portray the soft drinks Seven Up, Coca-Cola and Pepsi. Note I didn't say "sodas." That bit of transplant nomenclature grates on my nerves. Down here, some of us use "Coke" to indicate we're going to get a drink. "Hey, pull over to that store and let's get a coke." My Granddad Poland called Cokes "dopes," and I've written that Coca-Cola did indeed contain cocaine when it was in its infancy.

Highway 101 near Hickory Tavern, South Carolina, the old Mahon family store, according to locals.

That old Gulf Dealer sign, you just know, comforted many a traveler watching the needle hover over E. Easy to imagine an old wood-paneled Ford Wagon pulling in. Gulf Oil came to be in 1901. Red Man tobacco in 1904. Crush came out in 1911, and Moon Pies came out in 1917. Coca-Cola, introduced in 1886, is the second-oldest man in the room, second to Lucky Strike. These products bring to mind my grandparents' heyday. If only they could have seen how stores would evolve, for what strikes me here is what you don't see. No asphalt parking lot out back. Just a field of sheep sorrel and woods. Neither do you see mercury vapor lights. No rack for shopping carts. Paper, not plastic, bags worked just fine. For some of us, country stores bring to mind great memories such as pouring peanuts into a Coke bottle. As I often say in book presentations, "I can't see my grandchildren many years from now reminiscing and saying, 'Man, they just don't make stores like Walmart anymore.'"

As younger generations get all excited about the latest app on their phones, we older types circle the drain. Yes, times change. The Gulf Oil sign rusts and vines invade the store. No greeter stood in this store's door, beneath which a stack of bricks served as steps. You had to open the door yourself. No automatic opening to welcome flies. For now, it's here, and it brings to mind an e-mail a lady sent me about today's kids: "They miss so much with their faces glued to smart phones and such. Do they ever take notice of the world around them?"

I doubt they do. Few, I'd wager, realize that the old store would be more authentic with a rusty tin roof, but I do love its red shingles.

NOSTALGIC FILLING STATION

On a warm September afternoon, I was driving along Highway 76 in Laurens, South Carolina. That evening, I was to speak at the library on the discoveries you can make along South Carolina's back roads. As I drove into Laurens, I made a discovery of my own: the Nostalgic Filling Station. On my right sat a pristine Texaco filling station. To say I did a double-take is an understatement.

This jewel of nostalgia shines under the loving care of owners Rich and Cindy Kuhnel. Rich and I discussed his love for vintage cars and nostalgia. The building was a 1930 family-owned Gulf station. "Then it was a Pure station for a few years," said Rich. "Then it was a Texaco station until it closed around 1953 or 1954." Thus, do you see it today as a Texaco station. The pumps are 1948 vintage, said Rich.

Inside you'll see a 1954 Seeburg jukebox, an old pay phone on the wall and a racy touch from the past: pinup girls.

On the first Friday of the month, all roads lead to the Kuhnels' vintage station. "We hold a cruise-in then," said Rich. "Lots of people come here to take photographs of their classic cars," said Rich, who adds that 85 percent of the cars range from the 1940s to the 1960s. "We see a few hot rods, too," he said.

See the old station in person and you see why people love to use the Nostalgic Filling Station as a backdrop for photographing their classic cars. The Kuhnels painstakingly restored this old 1930 filling station, and it is a beauty. Apparently, the Kuhnels gather no moss. They keep on rolling and

1110 West Main Street, Laurens, South Carolina. On the first Friday of the month, drivers arrive in classic cars during the evening.

restoring. When Rich and I talked, he and his wife were busy restoring a 1960 Dodge station wagon. Pay them a visit. Make a Friday drive if you will and enjoy the procession of classic cars sure to pull in at 1110 West Main Street, Laurens, South Carolina. Go inside and see iconic entertainers Elvis Presley and Marilyn Monroe.

TEXACO STORE

My daughter, Beth, drives Highway 751 to her job in Durham, North Carolina, and one day I went with her. We left her home in Apex, North Carolina, and headed for Durham. Making our way over to 751, we drove by this old store, which I call the Texaco Store. Later, I made another trip to see the store up close. It's a sign lover's delight. You'll see the Texaco Star, a Route 66 sign, a hand-painted 7-Up sign and other vintage

ads such as a Bardol Motor Oil Additive Sign. The Black Cat Pure Matured Virginia Cigarettes is a classic. You'll find there's a market for prints of this memorable ad.

You'll find plenty to study at this "Texaco Store," and you'll get a glimpse into the past. Old hubcaps and old license plates take us back to an era when cars were much bigger. The handsome Texaco pump up front provides an eye-catching centerpiece. You come away from this museum of sorts on Highway 751 with the impression that driving sure has changed.

I love places like this old store. We owe thanks to the men and women who take the time to serve as self-appointed curators of what once made driving so pleasurable.

Do you expect future self-appointed curators to re-create versions of today's so-called convenience stores in the next century?

I don't. Why preserve such colorless, boring places.

P.S. It was encouraging to see firewood for sale on the honor system at the old store.

On Highway 751 near Jordan Lake, in North Carolina you'll pass this "museum" where the honor system avails folks needing firewood.

OLD POST OFFICE
TURNED MUSEUM

I've long driven Highway 378 to my family home in Georgia. I'd estimate I've driven it round trip eight hundred times, and I've seen that highway change. Three old country stores burned. Old filling stations shut their doors. Men leveled forests. A solar farm sprang up, and fast-food franchises popped up too. Highway 378 has long been doing its best to become just another road to somewhere, and then one day I saw this treasure chest of nostalgia: what appeared to be an old country store with a hay rake out front. I didn't recall seeing it until a friend back home, Ella Arnold, told me about it. I must have become blind, much like the opening to James Dickey's poem "Looking for the Buckhead Boys": "Some of the time, going home, I go blind and can't find it."

Many times I drove by this old post office turned museum blind and couldn't find it, but the day came when I could see again thanks to Ella. After passing it for several more years, curiosity got the best of me. I finally had to stop. I knocked on the door of the house next door, and a lady met me. I told her I was working on a book about the back roads of South Carolina, and she invited me in. Later, her husband led me to the old building, which he told me was once a post office. Walking over to this homemade museum, a lot of ads from yesteryear caught my attention. Lots of soft drink ads: round, disc-like Coca-Cola signs, NEHI, KIST Root Beer and Pepsi. Cigarette ads too: Chesterfield with its "Best for You" tagline, Camel and other signs. Coble Ice Cream, kerosene and "Gas 41.9."

A do-it-yourself curator brings beauty and nostalgia to drivers on Highway 378 near the Edgefield-Saluda County line.

He opened the door sporting a vintage Viceroy Cigarette ad and light showered across the past. A glance revealed the things farmers needed. Five-gallon cans of farm machinery lubricants: Phillips 66, Union 76, Gulf, Ford Hydraulic Oil and Havoline Motor Oil. Then I spotted things the home needed: an enamel wash pan, an enamel mixing bowl, Mason jars, Chase & Sanborn Coffee, Lord Calvert Coffee and what appeared to be an aluminum teapot. Cardinal Lighter Fluid and a tin of Prince Albert Tobacco made for a good pairing. Billy Beer added a distinctive latter-day touch to the scene. Just out front, an old hand pump stands as a reminder of times when you didn't need electricity to get water from the earth.

Where else can you find such a collection from the past? Not necessarily in a "real" museum, which is a tad highbrow in its selections. You'll find vintage advertisements and farm equipment in some restaurants such as Cracker Barrel. But if you make a Sunday drive down a country road, sooner or later you'll come across a homemade museum. Consider yourself lucky.

SUNDAY DRIVE REVIVAL

What's to stop you from making a Sunday drive? Take a look at a map of your area and chart a route that takes you as far from cities and towns as possible. Explore areas distant from interstates. Visit places off the beaten path, and you will not be disappointed. Back during the pinnacle of the Sunday drive era, landmarks and places with a fascinating history made great destinations. Seek out interesting places that reward those who resurrect that Sunday drive custom. Revive the Sunday drive. You'll be glad you did.

A SMALL-TOWN GETAWAY

A lot of small towns struggle. Some seem on the verge of collapse. Many downsize against their will, and many seem sad. You drive through them and think, "Just what do the people here do for entertainment?" One, however, transformed itself through art, and it makes for a great modern-day Sunday drive. The town? Lake City, South Carolina, a town first known as Graham's Crossroads. Make a Sunday drive here to witness a tale of men and soil, transition and transformation. Even better, drive to Lake City when its ArtsFields festival is underway.

Once upon a time, many a cigarette shot out of the earth in this region. And then a shadow fell over this land that grew bright-leaf tobacco. Reports, statistics and diagnoses arrived. Now, come autumn, much of the region sports a fluffy white coat, and tobacco barns trade leaves for cotton bolls as more Pee Dee farmers switch from tobacco to cotton. Tobacco's decline led to the demise of many a barn, and that left us some winsome settings. There, lonely in a flat field, stands a structure with unmistakable lines: an old tobacco barn.

In old tobacco land, beautiful settings charm the eye. Old farmhouses stand weary but prideful. Spacious fields stretch to lines of dark green woods. Along the edge of fields, barns—veterans of former glories, old warriors that they were—do time. Changing lifestyles imprisoned them right where they stand. Rusting roofs, exposed beams, curling tin and collapsing outbuildings stand as monuments to hardworking hands that work no more. Surely the hands that sawed and hammered these buildings into life lie beneath the soil they plowed with tractors and mules. The lonely splendor manifest in rusted tin 'bacca barns leaning away from the winds of change blesses the land with beautiful detritus.

Around these parts, people still farm tobacco, but its demise has forced many to find new ways to earn a living, and the little towns people depend on have had to reinvent themselves too. For certain, one has.

There was a time when Lake City was South Carolina's leading producer of strawberries and, even more noteworthy, the bean capital of the world. My first stop in Lake City, in fact, would be at the Bean Market, a warehouse converted into a cultural and community center. Back in Lake City's farming heyday, it was the site of the world's largest truck auction of green beans. For anyone who farmed beans, all roads in the South led to the Bean Market. Farmers flush with green beans and dreams of green flocked to old Graham's Crossroads. All aboard! Their beans headed north on the freight trains that rolled through Lake City.

As the economy rose and dipped through the years, Lake City became a place you passed on the way to the beach. And then "The South's Most Engaging Art Festival and Competition"—ArtFields—made the roads into Lake City a whole lot busier. As in Bean Market days, all roads lead to Lake City come April–May. At the Bean Market, instead of beans, you'll find offices and creative space for the people who help make ArtFields happen.

While the story of Lake City's transformation through art is still being written, it is known wide and far. ArtFields seeks to fill Lake City with art and events and installations of art in public and private spaces. Artists and artisans give talks. It's fun, festive and informative. Walk the streets and look for the round, fluorescent orange stickers on local businesses. Inside, you'll find art. The entire town embraces art.

At the festival's conclusion, the people's choice and judges' categories designate the winning artists. Artists find the $100,000 in prizes enticing to say the least, though the forum itself is compelling. People walk the streets from venue to venue. They can register at the event and vote for the art that most impresses. Nearly every aspect of ArtFields is free, but there are a few events that require tickets.

Philanthropist billionaire and Lake City native Darla Moore grew up watching farmers employ creativity to sell their crops at market. She never forgot that. Her own creative gardening project on her ancestral farm grew into an inspiration that resulted in Moore's supporting "The South's Most Engaging Art Festival and Competition." She wanted to see creativity spread throughout Lake City and its communities. ArtFields resulted, and other

Over one hundred feet tall, this fire tower serves as a gateway for visitors to Moore Farms Botanical Garden near Lake City, South Carolina.

blessings are on the way. Changes are coming that will lead to educational and technical opportunities for students and enticements to young professionals. In true gardener style, Moore is planting the seeds for Lake City to grow into a place attractive to young, creative entrepreneurs. She refers to Lake City's renaissance as the reinvention of a town, not a revitalization. She and staff and local businesspeople she assembled seek to draw on the culture of authenticity that has given towns like Athens, Georgia, a style and essence impossible to overlook.

So far, it's happening. Ray McBride, the executive director of the Community Museum Society, spent much of his day showing me around the festival in 2015. As compelling as the art is, I enjoy reading the artists' statements. It makes for intriguing reading. The art itself ranges from playful (an artist portrayed as a large white rabbit) to serious and startling.

One year's overall winner, Craig Colorusso, won $50,000 for his *Sun Boxes Mach II*, an environmentally interactive piece that used solar power to generate a rhythm that would take 3.12 months of continuous sunlight before the composition begins again. I stood in the center of his array, and a soothing, mesmerizing sense of calm enveloped me. Colorusso, who is from Rogers, Arkansas, says no two people will ever hear the exact same piece, as each hears the tones based on where they stand within the work. "All the tones are different lengths so as they are lining up, it's like a giant polyrhythm," said Colorusso.

Not long after meeting Colorusso, we walked by Joe's Barbershop on Main Street, and McBride related how Baby Face Nelson robbed $114,000 in September 1934 from the Lake City Bank, which sat where Joe's is.

I headed out for a walking tour of as much art as I could see. Walking the town is a museum tour. Art covers a wide range, and it's interesting to watch the people study the art. It's a good place to people watch and see how the town comes alive.

As a grand finale, McBride and I met later, and he drove me out to tour Darla Moore's stunning botanical garden. Having spent a lot of time on a farm myself, it pleased me to see how an old heap of abandoned car, truck and farm equipment formed a self-made sculpture. When you see that, the art and the botanical garden, you get a holistic sense of the power of pure creativity—plants, painters, portraits, photographers and photographs, pointillism, potters and more. It's all waiting on you.

"A" for agriculture. "A" for art. Both enrich the spirit. In *A Sand County Almanac*, Aldo Leopold wrote, "There are two spiritual dangers in not owning a farm. One is the danger of supposing that breakfast comes from the grocery, and the other that heat comes from the furnace." On the other hand, there's spiritual sustenance in seeing how a town and farming community invited art into its midst and prospered.

As for the old farmers in the ground, well, I suspect they love knowing that warehouses that held beans and 'bacca now harbor brushwork, bricolage, beauty and bios. I imagine, too, that the old-timers consider the beautiful detritus they left behind to be their contribution to art. For each collapsing barn stands as a mixed media of nails, wood and tin that inevitably will crumble into the field it once surveyed and become earth—that all-embracing museum in this region where transition and transformation above ground are the order of the day.

FROM ROSE HILL
TO BRATTONSVILLE

Whether you ever make a Sunday drive or not, Faulkner was right. The past is not past. It's hiding. Travel some back roads, and if you know where to look, you can find it. I did one cool day in February. My journey unearthed some of South Carolina's past, a past that's given us so much history, a history being further examined. I traveled to Rose Hill Plantation State Historic Site and Historic Brattonsville, places that draw back the curtains on a past overlooked by many. Interpreters Nathan and Sara Johnson guided me back to a time seen through a lens called history. I could not have been in better hands. I saw the past up close.

ROSE HILL PLANTATION STATE HISTORIC SITE

When you turn off Sardis Road into Rose Hill Plantation, look uphill through old magnolias and you'll see a plantation home. Closer in, you'll walk past a 160-year-old rosebush, a glorious thing abloom, a garland of pink roses amid jungle-like greenery. Rose Hill, indeed. You'll see a log cabin, freestanding kitchen and tenant home too. More than that, you'll see the past.

Park manager Nathan "Nate" Johnson, in his forest green, gleaming brass South Carolina State Park Service uniform, brings protocol to Rose Hill Plantation State Historic Site. Before coming to Rose Hill, Nate was a ranger

South Carolina's sixty-eighth governor lived here just off Sardis Road in Union County, South Carolina, as have one hundred varieties of heirloom roses.

with the National Park Service at the homes of Frederick Douglass, Mary McLeod Bethune and Dr. Carter G. Woodson, a fine provenance.

Johnson, proudly wearing his ranger's hat, delivers a synopsis. "By 1860, Rose Hill was a two-thousand-acre cotton plantation. Today, the South Carolina State Park Service protects a forty-four-acre site at the center of the former plantation. The U.S. Forest Service administers the remaining acreage as part of Sumter National Forest."

I look around and see thick forests in all directions, but I know that beneath the leaves and among the roots of oaks, walnuts and pines lies soil where cotton once grew. Nate continues, "As many as 178 people were enslaved at Rose Hill by 1860, making it one of the largest enslaved communities in Union District."

This history of cotton, slavery and the plantation's grandeur resurrect the antebellum era for many, but Johnson knows there's more to Rose Hill than that. "The site contains significant resources besides the main house. Many of the site's significant stories happened after the Civil War." To make his point, he brings up post–Civil War times. "Reconstruction is a richly documented period in Rose Hill's history that sheds light on the hopes, dreams, needs and expectations of freed people. Labor contracts, censuses, voter registrations, court testimonies, school and church records and militia enrollments are some of the documents we rely on to tell the story of Reconstruction at Rose Hill."

Some know Rose Hill as the home of "Secession Governor" William Henry Gist, the sixty-eighth governor of South Carolina, from 1858 to 1860. A leader of the secession movement, he signed the Ordinance of Secession on December 20, 1860, breathing official life into the Confederacy. That's the narrative many are familiar with, but history is multifaceted, and Rose Hill is no exception. Johnson's mission is to tell lesser-known Rose Hill's stories. Walking the sloping hilltop, he explains, "Oral histories from former sharecroppers and tenant families who once lived on the plantation have helped us gain insight into the history of Rose Hill during the early 1900s. Their memories bring to life the landscape, buildings, roadbeds and archaeological sites around the former plantation. We share their memories with visitors so they feel connected to the site's history and understand its significance."

I've been to Rose Hill thrice. I imagine that time when fields of white and green surrounded it. Back then, folks could see clear down to the Tyger River. The past Faulkner referred to hides here, but there's a plan to unearth some of it. Said Johnson, "Archaeology will help us discover more about the past at Rose Hill. We're preparing for an archaeological survey of the entire forty-four-acre historic site. Findings from the survey and other projects will provide valuable information that can be incorporated into the site's reinterpretation."

Ruins of tenant houses line an old roadbed. "By studying these remains and conducting oral histories with people who once lived in these tenant houses, we are gaining a deeper understanding of the changing landscape and evolving history of the site," said Johnson.

For the last seventy years, people have interpreted Rose Hill as a secessionist movement shrine or a window into the lifestyle of an upstate planter family. Change is coming. "A recent plan for reinterpretation aims to reinvigorate the site and help it grow," said Johnson. "Through community outreach, oral history documentation, in-depth research and archaeological investigations, the South Carolina State Park Service is engaging the public with difficult, yet significant, histories: slavery, Reconstruction, racial violence and terrorism and the continuous struggle in South Carolina to define freedom, equality and citizenship."

To see Rose Hill Plantation is to glimpse another time. Family records tucked into an old Bible. Neck collars resting on a handsome trunk. An old tin tub where folks bathed. The L. Rickets Baltimore piano in the ballroom merits a look. Close your eyes and imagine stately dancing to a minuet from an earlier century, for surely they did. Then there's the four-poster bed where Gist and the first lady slept. See the portrait of distant cousin Belle Culp, hair parted down the middle like Alfalfa. Walk into the freestanding kitchen out back. See its spacious twelve-tiered brick fireplace where cooking took place. In a tenant home out back in dim light, you'll see where someone pasted newspaper to the wall to keep out the cold. Look closely and you'll see a word: "cotton." Check out the old log cabin where someone patched its wood with mortar. Step back and see what looks like the eye of a gator in the woodwork. The imagination gets a workout here.

Johnson said Rose Hill's visitors enjoy the site's stories. "The site has a long and difficult history that helps us understand the struggle in South Carolina to define freedom, citizenship and equality. We tell those stories through the perspectives of the Gists, enslaved people, freed people, sharecroppers and tenant farmers, as well as their contemporaries. It's powerful to engage with history where it actually happened."

The new vision is to become "a plantation that uses its difficult past to help shape a better future." Thus, the Rose Hill team has been researching Reconstruction and late nineteenth– to early twentieth–century history at the site to incorporate it into their interpretation. "Part of this research has included conducting oral history interviews with former sharecroppers and community members connected to the history of Rose Hill," said Johnson.

"We're preparing for an archaeological survey of the entire site," said Johnson. "We're exploring how to open up the tenant house, which has been closed to the public for about fifteen years. We are also having conversations with the U.S. Forest Service, which maintains most of the former plantation as part of Sumter National Forest, about how to interpret and provide access to resources associated with the site, such as a cemetery for people enslaved by the Gists. Many of these projects will enable us and our community to better tell diverse stories of the African American experience at Rose Hill and surrounding area."

Visit Rose Hill Plantation. Nate Johnson, park manager, will give you a memorable tour and interpretation. "I establish the park's vision and set goals so that we can reach park and agency missions. We're in the process of reinterpreting the site to include all its complex layers of history and memory. Community outreach, collaborating with partners and raising the park's profile are at the core of my job. We want to get more people involved with Rose Hill and increase awareness of our site's relevance for everybody."

Johnson takes great pride in his work. As a kid, he loved visiting museums and historic sites, along with taking family road trips, reading history books, studying for social studies classes and listening to elders talk about the past. That fondness for understanding the past lives in him still. "I have always had a strong belief that we can and should learn from our past," said Johnson.

THE JOURNEY CONTINUES

With a bit of tailwind, it takes about fifty-four minutes to drive from Rose Hill to Historic Brattonsville. Not quite forty-two miles, the route takes us northeast to Highway 49 through Union, Monarch Mill—by John B. Long Lake—Lockhart, McConnells and a circuitous route over and around Draper Wildlife Management Area into Historic Brattonsville. Sara Johnson knows this journey well. She drives it five days a week. If you think she's related to Nate Johnson, you're close. In 2006, she and Nate worked at the Aiken Rhett House Museum in Charleston. Today, they're married and interpreters of historic sites. For Sara, it's Historic Brattonsville.

HISTORIC BRATTONSVILLE

You won't find barbed wire or metal post fences on the farm in Historic Brattonsville in York County. You'll find no anachronisms here. You will find split-rail fences in this place where you can step back in time at an eight-hundred-acre historical site, one of South Carolina's most important cultural attractions, part of the York Culture & Heritage Museum.

At the property's heart is the Brattonsville Historic District (National Register of Historic Places). It features fourteen original buildings dating from the 1760s to the 1880s. The buildings and cultural landscape reflect four generations of Brattons and the people who lived around them.

Sara Johnson works at Brattonsville as the preservation/restoration specialist. It's a good fit. "I decided when I was eleven that I wanted to be a 'historic preservationist.'" When Sara was in the sixth grade, she had to choose a cause to write a persuasive paper for, and she chose to write about the need to preserve old buildings. "I've always had a love for old buildings and a particular interest in historic building materials, so I chose to go into architectural conservation, where I would be able to work hands-on on historic buildings."

Well, I'll say here that Sara loves her work at Brattonsville. She works with property manager Joe Mester to oversee the preservation of more than thirty-five buildings, including original historic structures and historic buildings moved to the site in the 1970s and '80s, as well as reconstructed buildings.

"A lot of what I do is hands-on preservation—work that we do in-house with our preservation team and summer interns to maintain our buildings," said Sara. As an example, she mentions the masonry restoration done on the two original slave buildings where they restored historic wood sash

This old split-rail fence meanders along at Brattonsville. Pioneers needed few tools to build such fences.

windows. Sara also performs condition assessments and prepares scopes of work for preservation of Brattonsville's buildings, as well as other historic buildings owned by York Culture & Heritage Museums. She works with architects, engineers and contractors hired for larger projects like the upcoming restoration of the Brick House.

Dr. John S. Bratton built the Brick House circa 1843 but died right before its completion. A planter and doctor, Bratton was also a merchant. The Brick House, a combined residential and commercial space, housed the Brattons' mercantile store, post office and living space on the first floor. At some point, probably during the 1850s, a wooden frame was added on the back, a bit of a mystery. Why and when was it built?

Let Sara take you back in time as she recounts detailed store records from 1843 to 1847: "Cloth, mostly imported fabrics but also homespun, was the most frequent item purchased. Customers also bought 'tobacco, pens, paper, soap, spectacles, boards, sugar, 1 lott chinaware, 4 Breakfast Plates, nails, razors, straw hats and bands, buttons, butt hinges, looking glasses, snuff, coffee, teakettles, books (including a catechism and an arithmetic book), kidd slippers, tin buckets, Epsom salts, chamber muggs [sic], pocket knives, saddle blankets, twine & bagging (for cotton) and cologne.'

"You get insight into the people's needs in the 1860s and 1870s as well. From the accounts John S. Bratton Jr. preserved, it appears that staples (such as molasses, lard, etc.) needed by the recently freed men and women who kept working for the Brattons provided partial payment for work."

Want more insight into life back then? Records from 1866 list the following items for sale: "flax, children's shoes, soda, paper, a coffee pot"; "a seine, tobacco, a comb, a hair brush, kerosene"; "a wash basin, raisins, a soup ladle, a tin pan, a hoop"; "a water dipper, a boy's hat, lady's gloves, soda crackers, candy"; "mustard, hams, children's stockings, needles, thread"; "a handkerchief, a cravat, cheese, mackerel, hose"; "calico, laudanum, a spelling book, a padlock, bitters, a carpet broom"; "ginger, cologne, a lamp & wicks, a whetstone, a fine comb"; "matches, lemonade, a straw hat & band, and a shaker bonnet."

In 1885, the Bratton Store moved from the Brick House into a new, freestanding adjacent building built specifically for this purpose. At that time, the Brick House was modified to make it completely residential. New partition walls went up on the first floor, and the two doors that provided separate access to the store and private space were bricked in, moving the entrance to the center. The Bratton Store operated out of the freestanding store structure until 1915, when it closed and the last of the

Brattons moved from Brattonsville. The building burned in 2004. Only the stone piers and central chimney remain.

In the 1820s, most slave cabins were built from logs, John Bratton, however, used brick, a unique departure from typical construction. Some thirty years would pass before other plantations built brick slave dwellings. While time eradicated most log slave cabins, Brattonsville's slave cabins endure. No one knows why Dr. John Simpson Bratton built brick cabins in the first place.

Among Brattonsville's twenty-nine structures stands an old corncrib. You'll see much here. See the faux grain door, painted for filming of *The Patriot*. See the extraordinary brick slave cabins. Step into the old smokehouse and inhale fragrances of woodsmoke and salt. See its salted meat.

Great plans are in store for the Brick House. "We are in contract negotiations with a general contractor to undertake the restoration of the building so that it can be opened as a museum space," said Sara. "Only the first floor of the Brick House will be restored to its appearance from the 1850s through the 1880s. The rest of the building will be stabilized."

Restoration will include removing partition walls built after the store was moved to the 1885 building, restoring the original configuration of doors and windows related to the store entrance and building custom store cabinetry and paneled counters based on photographs of the originals. A hatch that once led from the store space into the full-height cellar (possibly used for storage of goods) will also be restored.

The store will carry things it would have had in the late 1800s, based on receipts and records of goods sold there. The historic paint colors, based on paint analysis, will be restored throughout the first floor and exterior of the building. A vintage look and feel will only get better.

Brattonsville's vintage appearance isn't lost on Revolutionary War reenactors who stage the Battle of Huck's Defeat, a Revolutionary War rallying point that eventually led to the Kings Mountain victory. At his own home, William Bratton ambushed Captain Christian Huck and 130 Loyalist cavalry belonging to British lieutenant Colonel Banastre Tarleton's legion, a dominating defeat.

So, history lives on at Historic Brattonsville. And what might Sara want you to know? "I'd like people to know there will be a lot of exciting changes at Historic Brattonsville in the near future. We'll open up the Brick House to interpret a part of the Brattonsville history that has not been a major part of the site's interpretation until now. The Brick House tells the story of the mercantile/commercial side of the Brattonsville community and can better represent the period following the Civil War when the store/ post office run out of the Brick House would have served other farming families nearby, as well as the community of tenant farmers that worked for the Brattons during and after Reconstruction."

Travel from Rose Hill to Brattonsville, step back in time.

EPILOGUE

I stepped back in time to write this book, and my trip down memory lane was a good one. I saw things we used to see on Sunday drives and daydreamed about the vanished Southland. Often what made those drives so memorable were surprises. Take an old storm shelter, for instance. Folks used to retreat to those when storms and tornadoes were about. Or seeing an old sawdust pile, as ordinary as that seems. Well, they are gone now.

One place satisfies my longing for the days of Sunday drive surprises. In Kershaw County, South Carolina, if you drive thirteen miles north of Camden on old U.S. 1, you'll pass through Cassatt. When you do, look for the old fellow standing by the highway. His name is Albert, and he's a mannequin, but he's no dummy. He's a marketing genius. Thanks to Albert, Cathy's Original Dolls and Produce is now in this book.

On my trips to Apex, North Carolina, I had passed Albert many times. One day, I couldn't stand it any longer. I just had to know why this old codger, stiff as a board, stood in a hand truck by old U.S. 1. I stopped and learned that Cathy and Dean Anderson roll Albert out by U.S. 1 each morning. Cathy makes dolls, and she made Albert to resemble a mountain man. For a while, she had made smaller dolls and placed them outside the store. "The sun was rough on them," said Cathy, so she decided to make a bigger doll she could seat on an old wagon. Well, after Halloween one night, she arrived at the store to find the doll's hands missing. "Someone had tried to steal it…probably teenagers." Yep, probably so. She and Dean decided that a life-size doll would be next. Welcome to the world, Albert, you with your mop for hair and beard. You with your old-world Santa's face and bronze wire-rim glasses.

Despite the fact that Albert's been hit and run over many times, they keep rolling him out. "We've replaced his clothes, hat and all many times," said Cathy's husband, Dean, who's a dead ringer for Tennessee's Phil Fulmer. Albert's a survivor, and so are the Andersons. They are pure Americana, throwbacks to the days when a Sunday drive down a two-lane highway never failed to disappoint travelers. My stops in Cassatt on old U.S. 1 take me back in time, and as long as I travel this route, I'll stop by to chat, buy some tomatoes and see what doll Cathy is making.

Long may businesses like Cathy's Original Dolls and Produce open their doors along the lesser roads. Cathy and Dean are Cassatt originals, and they've run their store for almost thirty years now. It was twenty-five years ago that Cathy began making dolls. "I sell more now than I used to," she said. Well, the credit goes to Albert. That old mountain man has a way of pulling in customers, and he sure had the magic touch when it came to luring a Sunday driver writer to make a stop. The South is vanishing, but you can still find it. All you need to do is make one last Sunday drive. You'll be glad you did.

Albert dutifully watches traffic on U.S. 1 in Cassatt, South Carolina. Cathy and Dean Anderson roll Albert out daily.

ABOUT THE AUTHOR

 om Poland grew up in Lincoln County, Georgia, and graduated from the University of Georgia with degrees in journalism and education. He taught at the University of Georgia, Columbia College and the University of South Carolina. He writes about nature and the South and its people, traditions and lifestyles. His work appears in books and magazines, journals and newspapers throughout the South. He's a member of the SC Humanities Speaker's Bureau. In October 2018, Governor Henry McMaster conferred the Order of the Palmetto on Tom. He lives in Irmo, South Carolina.

Visit us at
www.historypress.com